Thank you Michelle!   One happy baby

ISBN No. 978-0-9929038-0-0
First Edition 2014

Published by Cooke Publishing
Herefordshire

Printed and bound by Orphans Press
Leominster, Herefordshire

Acknowledgements

I should like to say a big thank you to my husband Stephen and my daughters, Hollie and Charlotte, for being so patient with me whilst I have channeled my energies into my passion for helping new parents with their new babies. A big thank you also to everyone I have met on the way to writing this book - without you and the experiences I have had, it could never have happened.

My thanks also to Delphine Steel, Selina Tollemache Hopkins, Nina Shaw, Liz Hurran, Helen de Witte and Helen Titley for allowing me to take photographs of your babies, which have been made into drawings, and thank you for believing I could write a book when I wasn't so confident that I could!

Huge thanks must also go to:-

Jackie Appel-malmaeus and Alexander. I know you have always believed in me. There are things you have said to me in the past that I have continually kept in my mind to give me the confidence to do what I am doing and to write this book.

To all of the parents and babies who have allowed me into their lives at that special time. You are all very special families and I feel privileged to have met you. I can't name you all but you know who you are.

To Judith and Tony Sharod for believing in me in the first place; with editing, proof-reading, photography and design, and lots of time spent helping to put the book together.

To Charlotte Cooke for help with the cover design.

Michelle and Graham Barber for allowing the beautiful photograph of Mia to be included in this book.

Marie Cooke for finding the time to sketch the lovely illustrations.

To my Mum, Ann Bownes, (for being the best Mum), and Jean Parry and Eileen Davies for taking the time to read through my early draft, and thank YOU for buying this book which you are now reading.

Enjoy this precious time with your new baby

This book is intended for advice only

Every child is different

Listen to your baby and
trust your instinct as a parent

Contents

Introduction

Congratulations!

Your baby is here. You have been preparing and looking forward to this moment for months. It's an amazing little miracle and you are holding the most precious thing in your arms. Although this is really exciting it can also be very daunting. The realization of this little being and its responsibility can be overwhelming. Your baby will rely on you for every need.

There will be times when you are not sure why your baby is crying, - why is he awake when everyone else is trying to sleep? Your baby surely can't be hungry as he has only just fed? There will be times when you feel exhausted and your baby wants to feed all evening. Every new parent goes through the same thing. Don't worry, it is normal.

I have been asked many times 'Why haven't you written a book?' Sometimes, when I have left them, mothers say 'What would Fiona do?' when they come across a problem, or when something with the baby is changing.

So I am putting my knowledge and experience of babies on paper in the hope that I can help many new parents enjoy their new baby and take some of the worries away. You don't have to stress about a strict routine, but at the same time I do believe that some structure to your day enables you and baby to know what is happening.

It gives you the confidence to care for your baby, and when you are confident, your baby feels safe and secure.

This book is to be taken as a guide and to help you find what works for you and your baby as we are all different. It will help you guide your baby gently into a flexible routine so you can do normal things like go shopping or meet someone for a coffee, keep appointments or go to classes etc., or just fit in with the rest of the family and older siblings.

Remember, there is no right way or wrong way to do things as long as it is a safe way. You will find what suits you and your family; remember your baby does not know any different, so relax and enjoy these first weeks.

My Background

I am the youngest of four children and I grew up in the countryside. My first nephew, my eldest sister's son, was born when I was just eleven and he lived with us for a while, so I was enjoying feeding and changing nappies at a young age. She went on to have two more boys, and I loved helping with them.

More nephews and nieces came along from my other siblings, and then at twenty two I started my own family. I had an adorable little girl followed two years later by another adorable little girl. I absolutely loved being a mum and thoroughly enjoyed those early years although there were times when some help would have been nice! Those times were very precious because before I knew it they were off to school, then all grown up.

While they were at school I worked part time in a veterinary ophthalmology clinic and you may think 'what has that got to do with babies?' Well I think even my experience caring for animals helped me because we communicate with animals non-verbally. It is all through body language, sound and expression, because like babies they can't talk and tell you what is wrong or how they are feeling.

After eight years at the vets I decided I wanted to study, so I did an access to higher education and covered all the subjects enabling me to apply to do a midwifery degree. Then I was lucky enough to be accepted at Staffordshire University. I worked hard on the wards at Shrewsbury hospital for three years looking after ante-natal ladies and delivering many babies, but I found that I really enjoyed helping mums with their babies on the postnatal ward teaching them how to bathe their baby, change nappies, supporting with breastfeeding and generally helping them. Three weeks into my very last term I felt I needed a break so I took a year out. During this year I found Maternity Nursing or it found me.

I love my job so much, and having been doing it since 2006, I have never looked back.

My midwifery background has helped me immensely with my role as a Maternity Nurse, and in having my own children I can empathise with women. I have now worked with many families and helped them to adjust and enjoy their life with a new baby. I feel it's a great privilege to be working with families at this special time and I would like to share my experience with you in this book.

For ease of reading I have referred to the baby as he or him throughout this book.

What I believe

I believe babies should distinguish between daytime and night time. Daytime is bright and has lots of sounds - all the normal sounds of daily life. Cars, vacuum cleaners siblings, television etc. (white noise), and baby can be awake and chat and play but also take naps during the day. All the noises are normal and baby will sleep through it.

Night time is dark and quiet and it's when we sleep. In the early days babies find night time hard to sleep, not just because they might be hungry but because it is quiet. In the womb it is actually very noisy. Your baby is jiggled about all the time and listens to all the outside noises; in the womb, the whooshing of the blood from the placenta through the umbilical cord to the baby and mother's heartbeat and all the noises from her digestive system. Then suddenly it's dark and quiet and still - this is quite alien to your baby and he has to learn to adjust, which he will.

I believe you can have a feeding and sleeping routine wherever you are and whatever you are doing. Your baby will feed at regular intervals of around three hours. I say this because I aim for a three- hourly routine but obviously if your baby is hungry at 2½ hours then he needs to feed or if your baby is sleeping and you are out and about, then leave him up to four hours. However, I would not recommend letting a baby go longer than four hours from the start of a feed in the day time. Your baby will sleep for one long period during twenty four hours and you want this to happen at night when you are sleeping, so I would wake the baby up during the day. Some people may think this is cruel but everyone needs their sleep and it's best for you all to have it at night. A happy mum, a happy baby.

Your baby will learn to sleep in the nursery, the car seat, the pushchair, on a bus, out to lunch, wherever you might be. If for example you have an appointment, you can adjust the feed. If you have to be at a clinic, the GP or a baby massage class, then you can feed half the feed before you leave the house or when you get there, then do what it is you are doing, and if baby needs more give him some more and he will sleep on your way home.

I believe bedtime is bedtime, so when your baby is about 5 to 6 weeks old, have a bedtime routine set in place and once baby has gone to bed, that's where he stays until morning. Obviously if baby wakes or needs feeding, tend to the needs and put him back to his own bed.

Babies should also learn to settle themselves to sleep too, so put them in their bed or pram in the daytime. Fed and settled but awake they will look around happily and go to sleep. Some babies will look around happily then cry, but just watch what they are doing. If they are crying with their eyes shut they are probably trying to go to sleep, so leave them. If they settle on their own they will sleep longer. Obviously if they are getting distressed, they may have wind, so lift them up, get a 'burp' then place them back.

When babies are newborn and tiny they need lots of cuddles and closeness, so don't expect too much too soon from your little one. Remember they just came from a tight, warm and noisy womb; give your baby time for adjustment.

From the Womb to our World

Adjusting to our world

During your pregnancy your baby has been very happy in your womb, and why not? Your baby has been contained in a warm environment surrounded by soft but firm muscles and floating in amniotic fluid. He has been feeding constantly via the umbilical cord from the placenta, gaining all the necessary nutrients and oxygen.

Just before your baby is born it is tight in there, and when he kicks or moves his arms, he pushes against the walls of the uterus which protects the baby from danger. It is also very noisy in there, as mentioned on page 3. Also your baby is constantly jiggled around when you walk or move, so it's no surprise that when babies are born, and we expect them to wait for food on a schedule, sleep in a quiet place in a large basket and get used to being where there is no motion, that this is actually very strange to them and they will cry. This is the time to cuddle and jiggle/rock your baby when he wants it - don't worry - it will not spoil your baby.

Most babies will adjust quite quickly within two to three weeks and fall into a three-hourly feeding pattern. However, some babies will want to feed small amounts and more frequently, and want more cuddles.

You probably know already, that as soon as you pick your baby up into your arms he will stop crying. It is not that he knows it is a cuddle, it is just the feeling of being wrapped in your arms, which feels secure and safe, and with a rocking motion your baby will easily sleep. It is like being in the womb. You can mimic this safe secure feeling by swaddling and placing baby back into bed.

Swaddling

I am a great believer in the swaddle and believe it is the reason why many of the babies I care for sleep well and settle into an easy routine. When they are born, they jerk their little arms and twitch whilst sleeping; this often wakes them up. They can also hit themselves in the face and have no control over these movements. This is called the 'moro' reflex or 'startle' reflex. Also when your baby swipes its hands across his face by accident it causes the rooting/sucking reflex and, of course, baby then wants to suck, so confusing you into thinking he is hungry or wants a dummy. When they were in the womb, if they kicked or pushed with their arms or legs, they would feel resistance of the uterus walls and this was a safe secure feeling.

Swaddling mimics this feeling and enables you to put your baby down into a basket thus causing them to feel that same safety and security, so you can get on with other things. Baby will also sleep better and longer because he won't be woken up by the 'moro' reflex.

Each week he will sleep longer, take bigger feeds and so sleep longer. Baby will learn to sleep anywhere, whether it's noisy or quiet. Enjoy these first few weeks of cuddles and be patient your baby will do what you want. Just don't expect too much, too soon. Give him time to adjust to this out-of-the womb world.

How to swaddle

You will need a large square cotton sheet or large muslin square. Fold one corner down so you have a straight edge and lay your baby on it with the shoulders just below the straight edge, as this will wrap around the shoulders and body.

The full swaddle with arms tucked down (this is particularly good for a fussy baby; baby may cry whilst you do it and may cry for a few minutes when you put him down, but he will go off to sleep and sleep well).

Example of full swaddle:

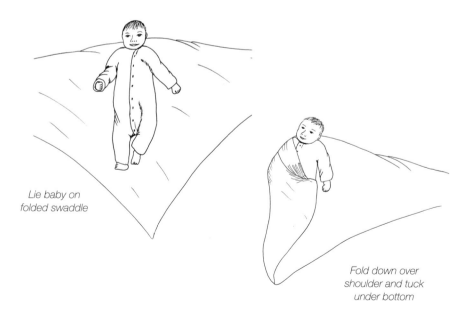

Lie baby on folded swaddle

Fold down over shoulder and tuck under bottom

Example of full swaddle:

Full swaddle with arms by
side, firm around arms,
but loose around hips
and legs

Full swaddle with arms across
chest (this is good for a more
relaxed baby who needs the
comfort but likes his arm up)

Half Swaddle

Half swaddle (this is good for a really 'chilled out' baby who likes to relax their arms above their head and isn't woken by the 'moro' reflex, or for an older baby who now gets arms out or gets hot).

If your baby is unsettled and will not stop crying you can swaddle your baby to mimic the tightness of the womb, jiggle them around a little in a continuous rhythm and motion and if they are crying loudly comfort them by saying 'shhhhhhhh, shhhhhhh' sound, like the whooshing of the umbilical cord from the placenta to the baby. This will normally calm a crying baby.

By one month to 6 weeks, your baby will have become used to not being in a dark tight place, being jiggled constantly, and will have grown out of this and will settle well in a crib. If you follow one of my flexible routines, baby will be doing the same thing roughly at the same time every day and will go down happily for naps and sleep times with no fuss. Your baby will know what is happening and know what to expect. I have worked with many babies that smile at me when I place them in their cot, as if they are saying 'thank you, I needed to go in here because I'm going to sleep'.

A newborn baby is completely different from a 6 week old baby so don't rush your newborn too much. Use these early days to get to know your baby. Hold him close, chat and learn your baby's language and 'cues' and learn to listen to what your baby is asking or telling you.

Many parents are in too much of a hurry to get baby into a routine. When they won't just do what you want right away, take your time. Every baby is different. Slowly guide them and it will all happen soon enough.

Example of half swaddle:

*Arms across chest, for comfort
or arms free with free movement*

Be calm and confident

Try to be calm and relaxed with your baby; if you are confident then your baby will feel safe and calm. You are the adult - your baby doesn't know what to do, he just wants to eat and sleep and poo. Your baby doesn't know that he needs to fit in around the other children or the appointments you have. You need to guide your baby into a pattern that suits you and your family. Babies can't do it on their own.

You will be given lots of advice from everyone and anyone. Take what suits you and ignore the rest. You know your baby better than anyone and you are the only one who can find what is right for you and your family.

Safe Sleep and Baby's Communication and Stimulation

Safe Sleeping

Research by the Foundation for the Study of Infant Death, now called The Lullaby Trust, suggests the safest way for your baby to sleep is on his back. Cot death is less common in babies who sleep on their backs. Your baby will not choke laid on its back. If the baby spills a little milk, he will let it dribble out of the side of the mouth. It is a good idea to put a muslin cloth on top of the sheet under the baby's head to save changing the whole sheet every time some milk is dribbled.

Lay your baby's feet to the foot of the crib. Baby's feet should be just touching the foot of the crib. This way he cannot slip down the crib/cot under the sheets and blankets. Do not use a pillow, just a firm mattress that fits well into the crib, covered with a sheet. To cover your baby, use layers of a sheet and thin blankets, NOT a duvet. Using several layers allows you to add or remove them depending on the temperature of the room where your baby is sleeping. Tuck the blankets firmly under the sides of the mattress so they don't come loose and move over baby's head. Tuck them up to the baby's shoulders.

The best way for your baby to sleep

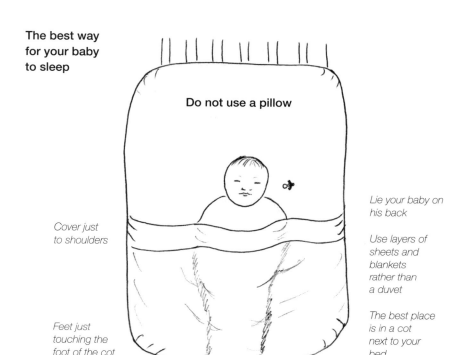

Do not use a pillow

Lie your baby on his back

Cover just to shoulders

Use layers of sheets and blankets rather than a duvet

Feet just touching the foot of the cot

The best place is in a cot next to your bed

When your baby is big enough or past 6 weeks, you can use a sleeping bag; this takes the worry of blankets away. Be sure to check the tog ratings on them so baby does not get too hot.

Babies need to be warm but not too warm. Being too warm increases the risk of cot death. Have the room at the normal temperature you would have it to be comfortable for you. Your baby is wrapped well in the cot so check he is not too hot by putting the back of your hand down the clothing and touching the chest. If baby feels too warm or sticky, remove some bedding or reduce the room temperature. It is OK for baby's hands to feel cold as long as the body is warm.

It is recommended that your baby sleeps in your room for the first 6 months. Studies also show that the use of a dummy reduces the risk of cot death but if your baby doesn't want it, don't force it on him.

Cigarette smoke is a main risk factor of cot death so try to create smoke-free zone. If you have smokers in the family, get them to smoke outside, but certainly not in the same room as the baby.

If your baby has any signs of illness, see a GP:

> If vomiting, especially bile or green vomit
>
> Takes less fluids and makes less urine
>
> High pitched or unusual cry
>
> Drowsiness, floppiness, or less responsive than usual
>
> Wheezy, grunting, fast or difficult breathing
>
> High fever or sweating a lot
>
> Looks pale or blue
>
> Blood in the nappies
>
> Rash

or if you just feel that your baby is unwell in some way, trust your instinct and get baby checked by a GP.

Cot death is uncommon but following the safe sleep guidelines will help reduce the risk further. It is rare, so please enjoy your baby.

Baby's communication and crying

From the moment your baby is born he already recognises voices. He will turn to the voice of his mother if being held by someone else and he will turn to the sound of the father too. Your baby has been listening to your voices whilst in the womb for months so he is already familiar with the family around him.

He will know the mother's odour, so will be instantly calmed when held by her.

Babies love faces and will mimic your expression. If you sit with your newborn close to your face, approximately 12 inches away, he will watch you intently. If you frown, he will frown, if you poke your tongue out your baby will poke his tongue out, but be patient, you need to repeat what you are doing and he will slowly copy. Sometimes you look away because you think he won't do it and then he does it.

Because babies love faces. They will watch with such concentration, really studying your face, which is why they find it so tiring. Also when they have had enough of looking at you, your baby will look away. This is a cue for you to stop talking to him; he needs a little quiet time. Sometimes baby will look back at you and you can continue your interaction, but if you continue to try and interact and baby doesn't want to, then baby will start to cry.

If your baby seems to cry more than some of your friend's babies, this is in no way a reflection on your parenting skills and it doesn't mean that he will always be difficult. You will need lots of support from family and friends and do take help when it is offered. Watching for your baby's cues is really helpful because you can anticipate what is going to set your baby off crying and change the situation to minimize this.

Cues to watch for:

Crying when hungry - you will soon learn that the cry for food is different from a tired cry. When a baby is hungry, the cry will start off slow and quiet, and will become louder and louder and will not let up until baby is fed. Your baby will probably have already been showing other signs of hunger before crying, such as poking out the tongue like a little lizard or swiping his hands across the mouth.

A tired cry may start off loud but will tail off with a half-hearted, 'can't be bothered' sort of cry.

Try and follow your baby's cues. This will make your life easier because you are listening to him telling you what he wants.

Looking away when you are talking, smiling or singing etc. means they have had enough. They are not interested any more. Sometimes they will also close their eyes almost like saying "I can't hear you". They may take a little break then turn back to you for more communication or they may just cry they have really had enough.

Yawning means they are tired - this is a cue to put them in their bed to sleep. If you miss this cue your baby will cry because he is tired.

When approximately 7 to 9 weeks old, your baby will also rub his eyes or face when he is tired, and then cry if you missed it.

Some babies at around this age will stop interacting with you and when you put them in their bed, they smile at you and become very chatty, as you have listened to them and they are saying 'thank you', that's just what they wanted.

Some babies will already be crying for their bed and need to cry themselves to sleep.

When babies are cooing and gurgling at you, try and make the same sounds back. They enjoy this. They think 'wow, you really understand me, let's chat'.

They really are clever little beings! Have you noticed how your baby seems to hate having the vest over the head, especially if the eyes are covered? He will grimace and wriggle and if anything is left over his eyes, will obviously cry, but he will bring his hands towards his head and try to remove the object. If it is left on long enough he would get it off his face, **but please don't try this at home.** The same thing happens when a hat falls over baby's eyes, he will wriggle until it's off and his face is clear again.

Babies love dark on light objects to look at. This is because their vision is still developing and dark on light is easier for them to see. They often look at pictures on a light wall or beams in a house. You can buy black and white cards or soft books for your baby to look at whilst he lays in his cot. He can watch this then drop off to sleep.

Crying is communication; it is baby's way of telling you he is hungry, bored, not interested any more or tired, or maybe just wants to see a smiley face and interact; or it could be they need reassurance that you are there and he is not alone.

Some babies cry very little and some babies cry a lot. This could just be down to their personality; we are all different. Some of us are quiet and some of us can be very loud. These are two extremes - most babies are somewhere in between. Unless there is an underlying cause for excessive crying, such as pain of some kind with a medical cause, then it is probably your baby's personality.

Whilst some babies are not bothered at all by noise or movement and are completely chilled out, some will happily sleep at any time, some will just look around happily then drop off to sleep, and others will cry or shout at everything. These babies cry at a nappy change, at bath time and might only stop shouting when his needs are met - such as being fed or put to bed - and even then he might need to shout to go to sleep, but when this baby shouts to go to sleep, he is just saying 'oh, I'm so tired I need to go to sleep and can't go to sleep' or 'oh, I'm so tired and will eventually fall asleep'. If you pick this baby up constantly when he is crying and trying to go to sleep, it will take longer because the 'I'm trying to go to sleep' cry is interrupted by you. Try and leave your baby - he will go to sleep on his own. If you were really tired, how would you feel if someone kept disturbing you?

We are all different; some people complain about almost everything and some of us are relaxed and take everything as it comes.

A routine of some kind allows everybody, including your baby, to know what is happening. You can be happy and confident that each day will be similar and you can plan around feed times etc. knowing what to expect from your baby and what to do next. Watching for your baby's 'cues' can help to minimize distress. Wriggling, grimacing, arching the back, yawning or turning away can be signs that baby needs to be left alone or be put in his basket. He may play and chat with himself then go to sleep. If you missed the first yawns then baby will become tired and will cry.

If your baby doesn't like being naked, then keep a towel or blanket over him. This will help him to feel secure. Try imagining yourself in your baby's situation and how you might feel if the same were happening to you. If he is jerking his arms and hands then secure with swaddle.

When a baby is over-tired they will jerk their arms and wave them around uncontrollably. This is not your baby getting active or excited and playing, this is over-stimulation. Your baby will then cry and won't be able to fall asleep because the body has become over-active and often if he is banging himself in the face or touching the mouth, this causes the 'rooting reflex' (sucking reflex) when he isn't actually hungry.

This is definitely a time for swaddling. I would recommend swaddling with the arms down by the side, so your baby can feel secure and can go to sleep.

Importance of cuddles and touch

I believe you can never give too many cuddles or too much love. The more love and nurturing you can give will help your baby feel safe and secure and grow to be a confident and independent child.

Don't be concerned that you will spoil your baby, there is no such thing. When your baby is born he needs to be close to you; he has been in your womb for 9 months. Your baby will soon learn to sleep on his own in a cot. There is time for that but in the first few weeks enjoy this time of closeness. They grow up too quickly.

To encourage closeness, infant massage is a great way to communicate love through touch, also when massaging your baby you have close eye contact which enables your baby to interact with you, however young.

'Being touched and caressed,
being massaged, is food for the infant.
Food as necessary as minerals vitamins and proteins'
- Dr Fredderick leBoyer

*Excerpt from Vimala McClure - Infant Massage - a Handbook for Loving Parents.
Souvenir Press, 2001*

The skin is the largest sensory organ in our bodies. Our body is covered with hundreds and thousands of sensory cells. When touched with massage the nerve cells start firing messages to the brain. This improves brain-body communication, and any stimulation for your baby helps with brain development.

Be aware too, only massage your baby at a time that is good for your baby, so when he has just woken or has fed and is in a happy alert state. If your baby is tired or getting tired, then a massage would be too stimulating and your baby will get upset. Watch for your baby's cues - if your baby does not want a massage then respect this and give it at another time, but if your baby has had all his needs met, a full tummy, not too tired, then he will probably love it.

'A daily massage raises an infant's stimulation threshold; babies who have difficulty handling stimulation gradually build a tolerance. High-need babies begin to learn to regulate the manner in which they respond to stressful experiences, which reduces the levels of tension they develop throughout the day. 'Colicky' babies are calmed and able to relax their bodies so that tension doesn't escalate their discomfort. A regular massage provides your baby with an early stress management programme that will be of value to them in years to come'.

As a Maternity Nurse I found that after bathing the baby, a natural thing to do was rub oil or a baby moisturiser into baby's skin. Think how nice our skin feels when we have moisturised.

Over a period of time I found babies loved this, so I learnt how to massage a baby properly and was able to do this through the IAIM (International Association of Infant Massage). I found the course truly amazing and inspirational.

I learned how babies who did not receive touch (those babies growing up in European orphanages in the 1980's, for example) did not develop well mentally or physically. Without touch and love. a baby or child cannot not thrive.

Research by Dr Tiffany Field on premature babies found that when massaged daily, the babies spent more time in an active alert and awake state, cried less, had lower Cortisol hormone levels, indicating less depression, and went to sleep more quickly after a massage than they did after rocking. Over a six week period, the massaged babies gained more weight, had an improved emotional sociability and 'soothability' temperament, had decreased urinary stress hormones and increased levels of seratonin (one of the brain's natural pain relievers). These babies left the hospital earlier than those babies not massaged.

This was enough for me to realise the true value of touch.

Benefits of massage

- Helps neuron/brain development.

- Enhances communication with your baby through touch, eye contact, and verbal response between the two of you.

- Produces feel-good hormones for both you and your baby

- Helps you bond with your baby, and can reduce postnatal depression. It is a joyful thing to do with your baby.

- Reduces stress hormones, so relaxing your baby, therefore helping them to cope better with reflux, wind, and constipation.

- Improves stimulation levels, enabling them to cope with more stimulation before getting too tired or stressed.

- Relaxes them, helping them sleep.

For further information on this subject of massage, read 'Infant Massage - a Handbook for Loving Parents' by Vimala McClure. Vimala is the founder of the International Association of Infant Massage.

Infant Massage is based on the tradition of Indian massage, Swedish massage, a little reflexology and yoga.

It is also worth going along to an IAIM class. There you will meet other parents in the same situation as you and it is a wonderfully relaxing class for you and your baby.

Since doing the course I am now able to teach mothers and fathers to massage their baby, and watch them enjoy those moments.

I remember once working with a family where I had taught the mother to massage her baby and suggested showing dad how to massage. He was a very busy and quite highly-stressed man - he needed to be this way for his job. I asked him a couple of evenings in a row, after baby had bathed, to come and massage his baby. He said 'yes' but was always busy. One evening he came in the bathroom, we sat on the floor, I had a doll, he had the baby and we started the massage. The baby was loving this as he was already used to massage. Baby was cooing and chatting to his daddy. It was amazing; I watched the stress disappear from this man, and he enjoyed this close communication that was happening between them.

A baby massage is of great value to fathers as well as mothers, particularly as they don't always have the same time with their baby, especially when mum is feeding.

Make time for this. It is a wonderful thing to do yet so simple. It is the giving and receiving of love and it doesn't cost a thing.

'When from the wearing war of life,
I seek release.
I look into my baby's face and there find peace.'
Martha F Crow.
From Vimala McClure, 'Infant Massage - a Handbook for Loving Parents'.
Souvenir Press, 2001

Hydrotherapy

Also as a Maternity Nurse I have taken many babies to The Baby Spa in High Street, Kensington, London. Water has similar benefits as massage as it stimulates all the senses. I have taken babies as young as 2 weeks of age and it is AMAZING how these little beings are so naturally relaxed in the water. The baby can be crying because you have just removed his clothes and nappy and as soon as the little float is placed under the chin and baby is placed in the water, peace and tranquility takes over. The baby goes into this unique meditative-like state. It is amazing to see the parents watch in awe as these babies behave in a way that you will not see at any other time than when they are freely floating in the water. They are watched carefully by the therapist, some of the newborns go straight to sleep but the senses are still being stimulated whist in the water. If they start to show any signs of stress or of being over-tired, they are gently removed from the water, wrapped in a warm soft towel and cuddled or fed by mummy, they then enjoy a gentle massage and often leave the premises sleeping soundly in their pram. Look up www.yourbabyspa.com, founded by the lovely Laura Sevenus.

Playtime/Activity/Awake time

When your baby is first born there is no activity time. The time your baby is awake to feed is it! So baby may wake up, cry for food, take half an hour to an hour to feed, then go straight back to sleep. Your baby will eat and sleep around the clock!

As the weeks go by, your baby will be more awake during feeding and staying awake for a little chat for say, 20 minutes afterwards. You may feed then put your baby back in the crib and he will happily look around, then either cry because he is tired or drop off quietly to sleep. By week three baby will have 'uncurled' and be happy to look around. Try putting him in a chair or under a baby gym, or tuck a black and white book in the crib to look at. Their attention span will not last very long. Some babies may gaze at something for only 10 minutes and be bored or tired and others will be entertained for longer. So if your baby is still wide awake, not yawning or showing signs of tiredness, but cries, he maybe bored, so move him or give him something else to look at. It maybe he wants a chat with you or a cuddle before going to sleep.

As your baby approaches one month to six weeks old, he will certainly want to spend much longer awake, so place him on the gym or under a mobile, but leave him to concentrate. You don't have to be the entertainer. I have seen many times where the baby is lying on their mat very contented, then mummy or daddy comes in and starts chatting very excitedly or shaking toys in their face and the baby starts to cry. This is because your baby is concentrating and you have created a disturbance. How would you like it if you were reading the paper or a book and concentrating hard then someone comes and interrupts you or starts shaking the book? You have to try and think like a baby. Before you know it your baby will be waking, eating, playing and then sleeping again at roughly the same times every day and you have a nice routine in place and your baby is very happy.

Kicking Slippers have a bell in for activity time

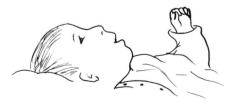

Baby will watch moving toys

Tummy Time

During awake time or play time or even massage time it is important to give some tummy time even if it is just a minute each day.

At first your baby may not like this but if you do it regularly he will learn to bring his hands forward and lift his head. This is good for strengthening the neck and back muscles, and as he gets used to it, he will be happy to lie on his tummy bringing his head up and looking around from a different view. Position yourself where he can still see your face; he may not like it if he can't see anyone or anything. You could also place a mirror for him to see the reflection.

Things you may need for your Baby

Baby Essentials

Feeding breast and bottle

Breast pump, one that mimics the natural suck of the baby. Quite portable

Breast milk storage bags, if you intend to express regularly

Breast pads

Nipple cream

Fitted nursing bras

If formula feeding, choose which bottles are anti-colic and are BPA free; there are many on the market

Steam Steriliser, or microwave steriliser, or cold water steriliser

Citric acid, to descale steam steriliser. Not needed for microwave or cold water ones

Clothes

Vests

Sleep suits, at least six

Cardigan, two

Muslin cloths, at least ten

Bathing and Changing

54 pack newborn nappies x 2

Cotton wool or water based wipes

Nappy bin

Towels, at least two

Barrier cream

Changing mat

Baby bath, or you can bath in big bath

Top and tail bowl

Sleeping

Crib/moses basket until approximately 4 months, depending on size of baby

Mattress protector

Fitted bottom sheets, at least two

Swaddling sheets, at least two

Cotton cellular blankets, at least two

Activity

Pram/pushchair. Choose one that is practical for you, there are many on the market

Car seat, Maxi-Cosi fits most pushchairs

Baby chair

Baby sling; choose one which is both supportive and not stressful on your back

Mobile; choose one with music, nature sounds and stimulates. This is used at awake times

Baby gym

Choosing a steriliser

Find one which works for you.

The microwave ones are small and portable and you can use them, wash them and put them away. They also sterilise very quickly - done in 5 minutes. Follow the instructions.

The steam sterilisers: there are many on the market; you need to leave them out on the kitchen worktop near an electric supply - they take from 8 to 12 minutes. Follow the instructions for your appliance. You will also need to descale them once a month depending on how much you use them.

You can also use a container with water and sterlising tablets. You need to change the water every 24 hours.

Once the bottles are sterile and using clean hands I suggest putting the bottles together so they are ready when you need them. This will also avoid contaminating the other bottles every time you open the lid of the steriliser if you are only taking one out at a time.

Dummies/soothers

I will just mention dummies. Some people love them, some people hate them. I don't like a baby to rely on one to get to sleep, but when a baby is small they like to suck. Some babies feed and when they are full, they are settled and will go off to sleep without the need of a dummy. However some will like to suck even when they are not hungry and if you are breast feeding, and you have the time and don't mind your baby on your breast constantly, then great, but a lot of mothers would find this tiring so I would say give your baby a dummy. Do what makes life easier - it may only be temporary. Once baby is feeding, in a reasonable routine and is more alert and playing, I would try to get rid of it.

I would get rid of the dummy at about 9 weeks. If it starts to become a problem, and your baby starts waking when it drops out, then get rid of it. When he is dropping off, pull the dummy out, or you can decide the baby is not having the dummy anymore and get rid of it altogether. At around 7 to 8 weeks your baby should have good control of his hands so he can suck his fingers or thumb when he wakes and soothe himself back to sleep. Also, he will not be so desperate for food like a newborn, so can learn to settle himself.

Clothing

Dress your baby appropriately to the temperature. If you are wearing extra layers in the winter because you are cold, then your baby will need extra layers. Vest, sleep suit and cardigan if necessary. When going out, put a hat on him and a winter suit if in a carrier, or hat and cardigan if in a pram, with two layers of blankets. Check your baby's temperature to make sure he is not too hot when wrapped so well, by placing your hand on his chest. Always remove a hat when indoors as your baby will become too hot.

Baby in warm clothing

Alternatively when in summer and it is hot, you wear as little as possible, so your baby may only need a nappy and vest, or just a nappy.

Baby in minimal clothing

Changing bag for out and about

You will need:-

A folding changing mat or towel or disposable mat

At least two nappies, obviously more if you are out for a long day

Water based nappy wipes

Barrier cream

Nappy sacks

A change of clothes, vest and baby grow.

Muslin cloths

Bottles of already measured water with measured powdered formula, or cartons of readymade formula, if using

A powder dispenser for formula

Soothers/dummy if using

A toy

Nappy Changing and Bathing

How often should the Nappy be changed?

You will need to change your baby's nappy every time he has a poo. If your baby is asleep and you know he has done a poo, obviously leave it until he wakes up. Baby will wake up hungry so it is best to start feeding. Baby will probably get sleepy in the middle of the feed then you can burp and change the nappy, waking him up to continue feeding.

In the early days, six to eight nappies a day is perfectly normal - you may use more or less. In the night, I would only change baby's nappy if he has poo'd, so try not to disturb him too much. You may think it is a long time to have a nappy on but when your baby is sleeping for 12 hours, you will not want to wake your sleeping baby to change the nappy, so don't worry; it's fine to leave it on if it is only urine. This is assuming you are using disposable nappies. If you are using cotton nappies, then use lots of barrier cream and change the nappy more frequently to prevent nappy rash.

What should the contents look like?

The first few dirty nappies will be meconium; this is very dark green almost black, very sticky and tar-like poo. Once your baby is eating well this will change to a lighter green then yellow. If you are breast feeding the poo will be very loose and a mustard-seed consistency and may smell quite sweet. If you are using formula feed, it will be yellow but of slightly pasty consistency and a little more smelly. Your baby should be passing urine constantly.

If using a changing table, **please don't walk away from your baby whilst he is on it,** even if your baby is newborn. It only takes a second for your baby to lift up his legs in to the air, lean to the side and roll off on to the floor. If you need to leave your baby, place him somewhere safe, in the cot for example.

Lie baby on his back on a changing area - you can use a large towel or changing mat - this can be on a changing table or on the bed or floor, wherever you can find that is suitable

Baby-grows or sleep suits with poppers down the front and inside of legs are ideal and easy to open and access the nappy. Undo the tabs of the nappy and peer inside. If baby has done a poo, then use the nappy to try to wipe most of the poo away. Use the front of the nappy to wipe downwards and leave the nappy there tucked closed under the bottom so you have a clean area. I only recommend the use of cotton wool to clean babies under a month and then introduce water-based baby wipes.

Put a barrier cream on the bottom area if it is looking sore, to heal and protect it.

For little girls wipe from front to back, so wipe downwards towards the bottom so taking soiling away from the vagina and don't be alarmed if you see a little blood stained mucous coming from the vagina; this is normal and called a pseudo period. However, if you are concerned speak to a Midwife or health professional.

For boys, wipe over and around the penis, lift testicles and clean in the creases. Under the testicles can get sore here if not cleaned well.

If your little boy has been circumcised, then follow your surgeon's instructions. You can put a little Vaseline in the nappy right in front of the penis so the nappy does not stick to the penis. Keep the nappy area clean as normal. You will be told about any swelling and what to expect, but always if you are concerned speak to your health professional.

Bathing

Safety first

Place baby on the floor or surface where he is safe and cannot roll off.

Run cold water in to the bath first to prevent scalding then add hot water.

Never leave your baby unattended in the bath, not even for a second. He could drown. If the phone rings ignore it; if someone is at the door ignore them or lift your baby out of the bath and wrap in the towel, place safely on the floor, or take baby with you in your arms.

You can wash your baby anywhere, in a sink if large enough, large bowl, baby bucket, baby bath or your adult bath if you can comfortably and safely lean in. Find what works for you.

There is no need to bath baby every day. You clean baby's bottom at every nappy change. You can wash baby's face daily and under the chin where milk may collect to prevent it getting smelly and sore. Use cotton wool and warm water. I use only water for the first month as babies' skin can be sensitive to harsh soapy products which can dry out sensitive skin

Bathing every other day is sufficient and even if it is three days or more, that's ok. You can still keep baby clean with a little wash using cotton wool and water. Once you have established a routine you might like to bath one day then massage the next.

Firstly choose a time in the day that suits you and your baby, usually just before a feed, or you may want to give a tiny bit of the feed so you know baby will be happy for his bath, then give the rest when you have finished. It can be any time of day but as your baby gets to 5 or 6 weeks, it is a good idea to incorporate it into the bedtime routine. A baby loves a bath as much as we do and it can be relaxing for him before bedtime.

Prepare everything you will need for the bath and have the bathroom at a warm comfortable temperature. Place a large folded towel or changing mat on the floor of the bathroom then place a towel, which you will use to dry baby, on top of this. Lay baby on the towel whilst running the water. Most babies love the sound of running water and often if they are a little unsettled they will lie on a towel happily whilst listening to it. Have a clean nappy and change of clothes in the bathroom too, so you don't have to leave the room. If your bathroom is not big enough for floor use then you will find your own way to bath baby. You can prepare baby in his bedroom on the changing mat then carry through to the bathroom wrapped in the towel, then back to the bedroom to dry and dress. Find what works for you.

When they are tiny they don't like being naked, so I would lie baby there still dressed but once they are a little older at 6 weeks plus, then they love to be naked. They feel free without the nappy on and can kick happily. Naked time is fun for a baby.

Prepare the bath water to a temperature of 36.5°C to 37.5°C, which is our body temperature. Test this by dipping in your elbow not your hand. When dipping your elbow into the water, it will feel warm on your skin, not too hot and not too cold. It needs to be as warm as our body temperature. If it is too hot or too cold your baby will cry. You can use a bath thermometer if you prefer. A warm bath is nice and relaxing. Also have the water deep enough to submerge his body in. Imagine sitting in the bath with hardly any water, it wouldn't be very pleasant. Babies love to be immersed in the water, and once they feel secure and safe they will let their body relax and float.

I don't recommend adding anything to the water for the first month, so as not to cause any dryness to sensitive skin, and water is sufficient for washing.

Wash baby's face with warm water and cotton wool, around the eyes and ears and chin one side then use a clean piece of cotton wool for the other side so as not to pass on infection from one eye to the other. Clean nappy area if it's soiled.

Lift baby with one hand supporting the head and neck and the other hand under the bottom. Pace baby slowly in the bath then remove your hand from under his bottom. You can continue to hold your hand under baby's head if you feel safe doing so or you can move that hand across so the baby's head is resting on your forearm or wrist and your fingers are wrapped around baby's upper arm. Wash baby from head to toe with the other hand. I am right handed so I hold baby's head in my left hand and my right hand is free to wash him. Let baby have a little float; you can gently glide baby back and forth in the water. They find this very calming and soothing. Bathe for as little or as long as you like. If you are in a rush then a quick dip in and out is fine but if you have time, and baby is happy, then both of you can enjoy the experience.

I tend not to use sponges on tiny babies. I use just my hands to wash, scooping water over the hair. They love this. Try not to splash the face. Wash under chin, arm pits, creases of elbows, hands, groin and creases behind the knees etc. If using sponges it is easy to forget which sponge you have used on the bottom area then next time it gets used for the face, which is not good, So if using them put them to be washed after each bath or have one colour for the face and one for the bottom area.

If you choose to use a bath chair or hammock for baby, then don't fill the bath too deep as baby will float and lift off the chair. Also baby's body is not fully in the water so you can cover his tummy with a flannel so he doesn't get cold or feel so exposed.

Don't worry about the umbilical cord. It is ok for it to have a good soak; you don't need to do anything to it, just pat dry around it when baby is out of the bath.

Lift baby out of the bath, one hand under the head and neck, the other under the bottom. Place on the towel you have laid on the floor and wrap him up (like a bug in a rug) covering the hair as baby will get cold. Dry baby from head to toe, not forgetting to dry the crease behind knees and elbows, as these can get sore if left wet. Roll baby on to side to dry his back. Once the umbilical cord has dropped off, which could be anywhere from one to two weeks, depending on the thickness, I then put babies on their tummies for drying and also when massaging. Tummy time is good to strengthen the neck and back muscles; baby will learn to lift his head.

There is no reason why you can't have baby in the bath with you or daddy. It's a lovely thing to do. Daddies like this time together too. Do it safely - get into a nice warm bath of again 36.5°C to 37.5°C and get your partner to pass baby in. Baby will lie on your tummy or chest happily. Place a warm flannel over baby's shoulders to keep him warm. As babies get older at about 6 weeks they will love a shower with you too. It is very stimulating for the senses and it could be activity time in the morning shower with mummy or daddy.

Bath time is a good time to give a massage as baby is already undressed, but again you can give a massage to your baby any time of the day when you feel like it or when baby seems particularly relaxed and will allow you to do it.

If baby is happy after the bath and will allow you to massage, then great go ahead. He might want a little feed of an ounce, or 5 to 10 minutes of breast, then you can carry on with the massage.

Once bathed, massaged, dressed and fed, baby will probably fall sound asleep.

Don't be alarmed if you notice little lumps under your baby's nipples if you are breast feeding them. The hormones will cause little breasts; this is normal in little boys and girls and will settle down and disappear.

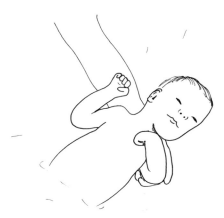

Head supported by wrist and fingers

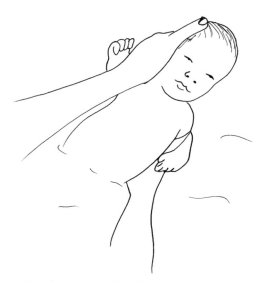

If you feel more comfortable, move around baby's upper arm and use your hands to support baby's head and back

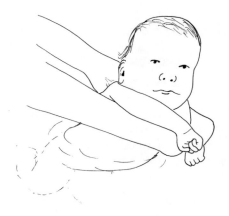

Baby supported in the water, keeping face out of the water

Baby wrapped warmly in a towel

Bathing with siblings

You already have yourself organised for bathing your older child, so now you have a baby to bath too. Why not bath baby with your older child or toddler in the big bath. He will love sharing a bath with his younger baby brother or sister.

Prepare the bath safely putting cold water in first then hot to a temperature of 36.5°C to 37.5°C. Don't add any bath products at this stage. You can add them after baby has finished. Have everything you will need in the bathroom with you. Baby can lie on the floor dressed or naked, if he likes to be naked, and can listen to the water running. Undress and put older child in the bath first and start playing, but keep things quiet as baby is going to get in once your older child is happy to sit in the bath and play with toys, bottles, sponges etc. Place baby in the bath by lifting with one hand under the head and one under the bottom. Wash baby from head to toe then take baby out. Place on the towel you have ready and dry, massage and dress. Leave baby on a dry towel whilst you continue with your older child.

So, older child is in the bath. You have never had to leave him and you have bathed baby, dried and dressed him and he is laying happy and safely on the floor. Now you can play and bath the older child, then get him out of the bath and dry and dress. This is just my example but you can, and will, find what works for you depending on your situation.

Evening and in the Night

Sleepy feed

Lift baby at 10pm-ish, but no longer than four hours from the last feed. If baby was fed at 6pm or 7pm I would lift baby at 10pm, still asleep and get baby to feed, burp and place back to sleep.

I never let a baby go longer than four hours between feeds during the day time. All babies will sleep one long period of four to five hours during a 24 hour period and ideally you would want this to happen whilst you are sleeping in the night. If you let your baby sleep a long time in the daytime hours then your baby will wake at night, probably three hourly, and you will not have a good night's sleep resulting in you being tired during the day. Also, allowing your baby to sleep later in the evening does not necessarily mean your baby will wake later in the night.

For example, you have been feeding your baby at 10pm for a couple of nights and he sleeps until 3am. So you think 'OK, tonight I am going to feed him a bit later, say, 11pm (I have tried this myself many times) and he will sleep until 4am', but no, he still wakes at 3am. So you have lost sleep by going to bed later and he still wakes at the same time.

Once you have established the daytime routine and the sleepy feed at 10pm-ish, your baby will generally wake at the same time every night for a week or so. This is easier to cope with than your baby waking at random times because your body gets used to it. He will then start waking at 3.15am, then 3.30am, then might surprise you with a 4am wake up, then go back to 3am for a couple of nights. However, before you know it, two weeks will have past and baby is now waking at 4.30am, then 5am and will continue to progress through the night until he has gets to 7am. Hooray, an all-night sleep. As a Maternity Nurse, I find the majority of babies are sleeping from 10pm until 7am by the age of 6 to 10 weeks if they are feeding well in the daytime hours, but don't worry if your baby isn't doing this, he will eventually. Be patient; baby also needs to be 10lbs (4.5kg) or over in weight to be able to cope a long time without food. Just be patient, all babies do this a little bit differently and in their own time, and if they were smaller at birth it might take them a little longer.

If, at six weeks, your baby is still waking early, or needing two feeds in the night, then he is not getting enough food in the daytime hours.

Also don't disturb your baby too much during the night feeds. Don't change the nappy unless there is a poo. Keep the lights low and try not to chat to your baby.

What if your baby is too sleepy for the sleepy feed?

Sometimes your baby goes into such a deep sleep at around 10pm that it is impossible to get him to feed, so what I would recommend is to try feeding half an hour earlier, before he is in this deep sleep. That way he will feed and you can get to bed early! Listen to your baby whilst he is sleeping; if at about 9.30pm he is still making little noises, then you know he is not in a deep sleep and will feed, but once there is silence, that's when it is difficult to feed him. After a couple of nights of 9.30pm you should be able to go back to 10-ish

What if baby won't take the sleepy feed or it makes no difference?

Some babies just won't do the sleepy feed; either they are too sleepy or it just doesn't make any difference.

If when they are settled at 7pm and are sleepy when you lift them at 10pm, and you have tried doing it earlier and later than 10pm, then leave your baby to see how long they will sleep.

If they usually wake around 3am having had the sleepy feed, then you leave out the sleepy feed and baby still wakes at 3am, then you might as well forget it. Put him to bed at 7 as usual, have a nice quiet evening and go to bed early, (or get a baby sitter and go out as you don't have to rush back for the sleepy feed). Hopefully, your baby will continue to progress through the night until sleeping 12 hours. Good luck!

Noises in the night

In my experience most babies make noises at night when they are sleeping. Some babies sleep very quietly and soundly until it's nearly time to feed, then they grunt and wriggle and can be quite loud but when you check them they are still asleep. So what I recommend is, don't go to them too soon. It might be another hour or so before they wake and actually cry for food. The longer your baby can go through the night until he feeds, the more likely he will then make it to 7am only feeding once in the night.

Other babies will wriggle and squirm and grunt all night long, so you have to learn not to listen to this and only listen out for the cry or else you will never get any sleep. So go to sleep, ignore the noises and wake up when they cry out through hunger and then feed them.

Travel

Travelling with your baby

Travelling with your baby doesn't have to be stressful. In fact whilst your baby is small this is probably the easiest time to travel. Your baby is easily portable, loves to be held and cuddled and doesn't need much entertaining, so will be easy whether being in a car, on a train, boat or plane. Don't let having a baby stop you from travelling or taking a holiday. Whilst your baby is small, he will eat and sleep and be content to sit or lie still. A toddler will need much more entertaining whilst travelling and will more easily get bored.

If you are planning on going abroad then your baby will need a passport. First you need to register the birth of your baby at your local Register Office, usually one in the area your baby was born. Once you have the birth certificate you can apply for a passport. You will need the usual passport size photograph of your baby's face with his eyes open, then send off your application form, which you can get at the Post Office. The Post Office will provide a service to help you fill out the forms and you can get a fast-track passport if you are intending to travel soon after the birth.

When booking your holiday make sure it is child-friendly. Even though your baby is small and not mobile yet, you need to be able to get out and about with the pushchair or pram, so avoid accommodation with lots of steps. Make sure there is easy access with a pushchair to sun terraces, pools and restaurants etc.

When booking a flight or train ticket, you won't need a seat for your baby as baby will be held in your arms or across your knee. If it is going to be a very long journey it may be worth booking the seat next to you so your baby can at least lie down, or you can take the car seat and strap baby on the seat. You can book seats where they have a bassinet for you to use, which is just in front of your seat.

Check with the airline and train service as to whether you can take car seats with you.

You will be able to take the pram or pushchair on the train but when flying you will need to leave it at the plane door and it will be waiting for you as soon as you land and disembark from the plane. On some occasions it may not be at the door but don't panic, it will arrive on the carousel with the luggage.

Families with young children or babies are usually asked to board first, so this gives you the time to get settled on the plane and prevents waiting in a queue any longer than is necessary.

Be prepared with feeds; if you are breast feeding then there is no problem. You will be able to feed baby wherever you feel comfortable. If giving bottles, take readily measured amounts of powder with you, as you may not be able to take liquids through security. You can ask for cooled boiled water once you are on the plane.

I would recommend having at least 2 bottles already prepared with water (for other than when you are on a plane), so that you have it ready whenever your baby wants to feed. If you have baby bottles with water in and you have been allowed to take it on the plane, be aware that when the cabin pressure changes, your bottles may leak, so loosen the lids to allow the air to escape, and keep upright to prevent leakage.

If you are breast feeding, remember to drink plenty of water to keep yourself hydrated. It is easy for several hours to go by and you realize you have not eaten or drunk anything.

When changing your baby's nappy whilst on the plane, you can do it either on your knee or across the seat next to you, if it's free, or you can place the changing mat on your partner's knee and change the nappy with your back to the aisle. No one will even know you are doing it.

Of course, there are baby changing facilities in the toilets if you prefer. Often there is a queue, but don't worry if people are waiting outside. You need the toilet and your baby needs a clean nappy and needs to be comfortable too.

One very important tip

Try to time it so that your baby feeds when taking off, then feed baby again when landing. This will prevent your baby's little ears from hurting.

It doesn't matter when you fly, whether its day or night but whatever time it is, try to stick to what is normal for your baby. Obviously you will have to adjust a little whilst you are travelling. So if you travel at night when your baby is normally sleeping, then don't disturb baby too much, and keep him sleeping. Lift baby out of bed, loosen the blanket or sleeping bag and place in the car seat. The same when you get to the airport or station. Transfer to pushchair with minimum disruption to sleeping baby

If it is daytime, then try to feed at normal times, but keep a little of the feed for take-off. Be prepared for the routine to go a little 'off sync'. Your baby may snack a little whilst travelling, but this is ok. The first 24 hours may be off schedule, but as soon as you arrive at your destination change your clock (if abroad) then try to adjust baby's routine to get back on track at the new time. You will find that baby will adjust easily and do the same when you travel back home.

If you are going somewhere hot, be sure to keep your little one in the shade and out of the sunshine. Their delicate skin will burn very easily.

You can drape a large muslin cloth all over the pushchair or pram or you can buy a large canopy that will stretch over the pram and will keep the sun off your baby. You may also need an insect or mosquito net, depending to where you are travelling.

What to pack for your baby:

Travel bag or hand luggage for your baby

Changing mat (fold up) or disposable changing mat

Nappy wipes

6 x nappies depending on length of journey

Change of clothes, 2 x vest and 2 x sleep suits

2 x soother/dummies if you use them.

2 x bottles with water if needed

2 x empty sterilised bottles

Measured amounts of powdered formula for enough feeds for 24 hours, in a dispenser. Be prepared, just in case of delays

2 x muslin cloths

Rattle or favourite toys, depending on age

Blanket, it can be cold when travelling with air conditioning

Sun glasses and hat, for when you arrive in the bright sunshine

Pushchair or pram, an easily folding one and lightweight

Enough nappies and wipes for the time you are away

Enough powder formula for the time you are away

At least four bottles, you can re-sterilise as you go

Your baby's own bedding and favorite toys

If you are taking a 'moses' basket, then you can squeeze in a bouncy chair and activity play gym too. You can book this in as baby equipment or extra luggage. Speak to the airline beforehand, to check what is allowed. Some hotels or villas will supply cots and sterilisers, so check this out too. It will save you having to take too much equipment.

You can use a travel steriliser which sterilises one bottle at a time with water and sterilising tablets. It is very small and won't take up much space in your suitcase. You can also use microwave bags which hold one or two bottles - you put some water in and the bottles in and seal the bag and pop it in the microwave for the recommended length of time. Obviously you will need to check if there is a microwave available if you choose this option.

Try not to over-pack, although you will need clothing for everyday of the week. If there are laundry facilities, then one week's supply is enough.

Travel first aid or medicine kit

Thermometer

Infant Paracetamol, only for infants over 2 months

Insect repellant

Insect bite cream or calamine lotion

Rehydration sachets for babies in case of vomiting and diarrhoea

Plasters

Antiseptic wipes

If you are travelling by car, you will need to take the same equipment. This may be less stressful for you if you worry about being around other people. You can please yourself what time you leave, what time you stop and take breaks etc., but the good thing about travelling with a baby is that they tend to sleep a lot as they love the feeling of motion. However you choose to travel, enjoy it!

Yourself and Your Family

Taking care of yourself

I cannot stress this enough. It is really important that you look after yourself. You are no good to anyone, including your baby and your husband, if you are exhausted. Make sure you get rest when you can. Have a drink and a snack in the morning if you can't face breakfast then go back to sleep. If you don't have to start your day early then stay in bed. For the first few weeks, your baby will eat often but will sleep quite a lot so take this time to recover to the adjustment and excitement of having a new baby in the house.

Some women are on a complete high after the baby is born but this adrenaline soon wears out and you can suddenly feel very tired. Try and eat breakfast, lunch and dinner and a snack in between. Eat healthily, so you have lots of energy, but if you are craving sweet things, then have it if your body is asking for it, and remember to drink plenty of fluids too, to keep from getting dehydrated, as this itself can make you feel tired.

So many times I have heard 'I have not had time to shower' or 'the baby won't sleep'. Your baby doesn't need to be sleeping for you to get anything done. Once your baby is fed and changed put him somewhere safe in his basket or chair and go and take a shower. He won't go anywhere and if he is unsettled, take him in the bathroom with you where at least you can still see him; babies love the sound of running water. He will probably be quite happy in there with you.

Let your baby get used to being in their basket awake. He will look around then drop off to sleep or may start to cry when getting tired, but will then go to sleep.

Do as much as you can whilst baby is awake; you don't have to be playing and entertaining your baby all the time. Watching you eat your breakfast is enough entertainment for your little one then you can enjoy a rest or some time to yourself whilst he is sleeping. In fact over stimulation of your baby is a cause for a cranky baby. They love smiley faces and chatting but tire very easily.

Accept help when it's offered. Anyone who has had a baby knows how tiring it can be, so if someone offers to load the dishwasher or hang out the washing etc., then let them. They genuinely want to help. They would not offer if they didn't want to, and it's a few less things for you to think about.

When your baby arrives you will have endless visitors. Everyone wants to see you and the new baby, but visitors can be very tiring so don't feel pressured to see everyone if you are not ready. Arrange visits when it is a good time for you - maybe when the baby is feeding so at least you are sitting, and both you and baby are awake. Also don't tire yourself by making lots of tea and biscuits; relax, show them where the kettle is and they can make you one. Your friends and family won't mind. They will want to help you.

Try and get your partner or family to help you keep on top of the housework but please don't stress about it. You and the baby are the important ones, the housework will still be there tomorrow and if you do find time to do it, it will still be there tomorrow too!

Siblings

Depending on the age of your child will depend on when and how you tell them that they are having a new baby. I don't advise telling them too early, as the time to wait for the baby will be too long and if your baby bump is not very big they may not understand.

If your child is 2½ years old or younger, they will adjust well to a new baby. They may demand your time a little more, but after a week or so it will be like the baby has always been there. If your child is a little older, they will be able to understand what is happening but may not adjust easily, as they have always had you to themselves and may find it difficult to share your time with the baby. Keep them informed and involved and it will be a normal progression for your family.

When your bump is visible it will be easier to explain. Tell your child that you are having a baby. Explain that it is inside your tummy and let them put their hands and ears on it to try and listen and feel your baby. It is far easier to understand if they can see something happening to your body. Tell them the baby is inside you and will be coming out soon.

If your child has some little friends who already have brothers or sisters this will be easier for them to understand.

There are children's books you can buy where the story is about the arrival of a new baby brother or sister, and reading these stories will help prepare for the baby too. Get your child involved as much as possible with the preparation of the nursery, getting the crib ready and preparing the pram, baby clothes etc.

When your baby is due, have arrangements in place as to who is caring for your child, maybe they can stay with grandma and grandpa or someone can stay at your house. Try to keep things normal, try not to fuss and worry too much, your child will adjust just fine. He has to, you can't send the baby back!

When your baby is ready to be born it is important you tell your child what is happening, that the baby is ready to be born and come out of your tummy and if you are going to hospital, explain where you are going and you may be there for a few days and as soon as the baby is out of mummy's tummy, he can come and see you and the baby. I feel that for them to come and see you at the hospital with the new baby is important. It gives your child the chance to meet his new baby brother or sister and then they go home with daddy leaving you and baby behind. The older child then is able to chat with daddy about it and is able to process what is happening before you come home with the baby.

Without this it can be quite a shock for mum to disappear and come back with this new baby when he wasn't expecting it.

Don't hide things from your child. It is a big shock to little ones when they don't know what is happening. Even if your child is still very young, explain everything; you will be surprised at how well he will cope with all this information.

Some parents buy a little gift for the older child from the new baby. This is a positive thing about the new baby coming. You can get a little dolly and crib for them to play with beforehand and show them pretend nappy changing and feeding and how we are gentle with a baby and baby doll.

Once your baby is home try to keep things as normal as you can. Leave baby to sleep and tend to your older child. When baby needs to feed let the sibling watch closely. Explain what is happening, let them help when nappy changing, get them to fetch things or pass things to you and let them hold the baby if they want to.

Sit them safely on the couch or bed and place baby on their lap. They will put their arms around them, tell them to be gentle. Once they have held them for a very short time they will push baby back to you and will have had enough. As long as you don't push the elder child out and say 'don't do this', 'don't do that' and make it fun and positive for them to have a brother or sister, they will accept it.

You can read stories to your elder child whilst you are feeding the baby. Have them play with puzzles close to you. Keep them informed and involved, and they will soon forget what it was like before the baby arrived.

Remember, the second child is very different from the first. You will find that your eldest child takes up most of your time and the baby just slots in.

Remember to teach the older child to be gentle and caring with the baby.

Never leave your elder child alone with your baby at first, as you are not sure how he will react around him. Children can forget and be quite rough and there could be some jealousy issues, so if you leave them together in the room, it shows that you trust the elder child, but watch them from the door so you can see how your older child is with the baby when he thinks you're not around.

Some children will carry on playing with their toys, oblivious to the fact there is a new baby. Another child will take any opportunity to bang baby on the head with a favourite toy, so be careful and aware that this can happen. Most older children are surprisingly gentle with a new baby.

Keep things normal. Don't over compensate your time for the older child. They have to accept you have to sometimes feed and change baby and that baby is here to stay.

Overall, if you are honest and talk to your child and answer questions appropriate for their age in a way that they understand, there shouldn't be any problems. They will love having a little baby brother or sister.

Pets

Ultimately make sure your baby is safe. Never leave your baby unattended with a cat or dog or any other pet that could harm your baby.

Keep good hygiene; wash your hands after handling pets or cleaning poo or cages, litter trays etc. Disinfect work surfaces when preparing baby bottles and foods.

Dogs and cats are like older children. They have had you to themselves until now and you probably have treated them like your babies, but now the new baby is here. Try not to push them out as they can react like a jealous child and you don't know how they might react. A dog or cat will be inquisitive when you bring your baby home. Your baby will smell of you so your pet will know it is family. If your pet wants to sniff your baby, let them, under your supervision, and keep your baby safe.

Cats like to curl up and sleep in nice warm places and a baby's crib or pram would be perfect for this, so make your crib safe with protective netting or shut the cat out of the room where your baby is sleeping, if you can't be watching them.

A dog will quickly learn not to jump up or lick your baby, but however much you trust your dog, whatever breed, never leave them alone with your baby. You can never quite trust how your dog will react when your baby is crying. The animal may not be bothered by the crying, or they might be scared by it, or may just try to look at your baby and jump up on it, so your baby could come to harm even unintentionally.

There have been many stories in the media over the years where dogs have attacked a child or savaged a baby, so the answer is **NEVER** leave a dog unsupervised with your child or baby.

Twins

With twins you have to be far more organised or you would never have any time to yourself. If you allowed the babies to do their own thing, one would wake up and feed - it may take an hour or so to feed and settle - and then the other one would wake. By the time you have fed and settled the second baby, it will be time to feed the first one and on it would go.

When one baby wakes I would start to feed that one and then when he seems happy I would put him somewhere safe. Then wake the other one and start to feed. When that one is settled, I would place him somewhere safe - on the bed or in a chair - then I would change the first one, finish feeding and settle in the chair or if sleepy put to bed, then change the second one's nappy, finish feeding and settle to sleep. This way they are always awake at the same time, maybe 20 minutes apart, and always sleeping at the same time. So you get a break.

The other option is when one wakes, wake the other one too and feed them together. You can prop them up on pillows and breast feed them together or you can sit them in a chair and bottle feed them at the same time. When they are both settled, burp and change nappies, then finish feeding and settle back to bed together.

There will be times when you have to feed together as they will both sometimes wake hungry at the same time. It's surprising how you learn to handle two babies at the same time. Usually with twins, one is patient and one is more demanding, so that helps. The more demanding twin always jumps the queue and the patient one allows it and doesn't care.

Sleeping - I allow the babies to sleep together in the daytime if in a basket and I separate them at night, but if you have them sleeping in a big cot they can share this from birth until they are too big or moving around too much. After all they have been together for 9 months and they like the closeness. First of all, when they are tiny, you can place them side by side. As they grow, you can put them at opposite ends with their feet at the ends and their heads almost meeting in the middle. Eventually they have to go in their own cots. At some point they may start to wake each other too but this is more likely to be when they are about 3 months old. Babies are all different you have to find what works for you and your babies.

There are many pushchairs on the market, side by side or one in front of the other. I have found that it is useful to find one that folds easily, but if you have space and don't need to be putting them up and down, then go for a sturdier one. It also depends if you are in the town or the country, or have steps, so have someone help you at the shop when you are buying your twin pram or buggy. I think it is as important as buying a car.

You will need double of everything on my list and take help whenever it is offered. When you have learned to handle one you can manage another one but obviously, it is more work, so accept help when it is offered. You will find you will have a lot of attention when you have twins; everyone is amazed by them. You can't go for a walk without someone speaking to you. Enjoy it! It's double the fun.

You can follow the same routines that I have put in place for single babies. Feeding the babies together or parting them by 20 minutes to half an hour.

Feeding

Burping - bringing up wind

It is important to burp your baby well after he has fed and before going to sleep, if he is to settle well and sleep well. Breast fed babies tend to take in less wind than a bottle fed baby but you still need to burp them.

Let your baby feed for as long as he likes on the breast or with the bottle. Don't stop him; your baby will stop feeding when he is ready. When baby stops eating, sit him upright; as long as his back is nice and straight and upright a burp should come.

You can sit your baby up straight on your knee or place over your shoulder.

When sitting on your knee, try pushing baby forward a little but don't bend the baby over, if you bend baby over too far at the waist, he is likely to bring back some milk. This is called a posset. A little positing is quite normal. Projectile vomiting, if it is a one off, is ok, but if this happens frequently or almost every feed then you should consult a doctor. The muscle which shuts at the top of the stomach is often weak in a newborn and allows milk to spill back, but if it is excessive amounts of milk, the muscle may be weaker than normal so it would be best to get it checked out.

There is no need to spend hours trying to get a burp from your baby. In my experience if your baby hasn't burped almost straight away after feeding, he probably doesn't need to or it just isn't ready to come. When you have finished feeding and settled your baby down to sleep, if he has wind then it will be uncomfortable for baby to lay flat so he will wriggle and cry out, so lift your baby up and he should burp easily; then you can put baby back down to sleep.

If you think your baby is gulping and taking in lots of air when bottle feeding you can buy anti-colic bottles which are designed to stop your baby gulping so much air when feeding.

If you are breast feeding you can try to eliminate certain foods that you eat that you think maybe causing wind, e.g. tomatoes, strawberries, kiwi fruit, grapes or anything acidic, or if your baby is struggling to break down lactose you could try cutting down on dairy products but don't change your diet unless you think there is something wrong and consult your GP or Health Visitor.

When burping your baby, think of the wind or gas as an air bubble and bubbles travel upwards so you need your baby's oesophagus to be straight (the tube from baby's mouth to the stomach), so that the bubbles can travel upwards and out through the mouth.

If the bubbles have gone the other direction downwards, it will pass along the intestine and this can sometimes be uncomfortable for baby but it will pass out of his bottom.

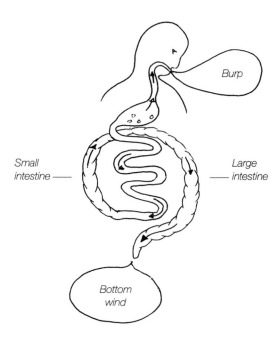

Diagram of air travelling upwards and downwards

Burping position
Supporting the chin, chest and back

How are you feeding your baby? Breast or bottle?

This is purely your choice and you should not be made to feel guilty whichever you choose. You should do what feels right for you. *Remember a happy mum, a happy baby.*

I would encourage you to try breast feeding. How will you know what it's like if you don't try it? If it works for you and you enjoy it, then great. There are many benefits to breast feeding in the early days. It is made up of all the right nutrients for your baby – it is the right temperature, it is free and readily available and it is very easily digested. It also helps move the meconium through your baby's digestive system and has antibodies which are good for your baby's immune system.

With the right support I have found, even where there are problems they can be overcome, and mums are able to continue to feed their baby. Please don't stress about it if you can't breast feed or choose not to. Generations have been brought up on 'formula milk', and are just fine, very happy and healthy.

Let us compare the two:

Bottle feeding

Advantages	Disadvantages
Anyone can feed your baby You don't have to worry about breast feeding in public You can see how much your baby is drinking Baby feeds quickly	You have to sterilise and make up bottles You have to pay for it You have to throw it away if not used If not sterilised or kept at the wrong temperature can cause stomach upsets Babies can take in air from the bottle and cause wind

Breast feeding

Advantages	Disadvantages
It's always available	Can get engorged and painful breast
It's the right temperature	Sore nipples
It is made especially for your baby and has all the right nutrients	Only you can feed the baby
	Can be time consuming
It has antibodies to boost immune system	Can be tiring
It's easily digested, less windy for your baby	You may not like feeding in public places so it limits where you go
It's free	
It produces hormones which help you relax	
Has health benefits to the mother and the uterus contracts quicker	
You use calories to feed your baby	
May prevent some women cancers?	
May prevent osteoarthritis/perosis	

Breast Feeding

Anatomy and Physiology

Make sure your baby eats well.

In my experience crying in the early days is almost always about hunger. I am going to talk in-depth about breast feeding, so if you have chosen to 'formula' feed and don't want to read this section, go straight to the section for bottle feeding with formula.

The shape and size of your breast really doesn't matter. When it comes to feeding your baby you can be flat chested and your breast will still make enough milk for your baby. Large breasts will also make enough milk for your baby. The size of your breast is no indicator as to how much milk you will produce.

I believe it is important for you to understand how your breast produces milk so you can feel confident when feeding your baby. It's not like a bottle where it is just full or empty; your breast continues to make milk, so even when they may not feel as full at the end of the feed as they did at the beginning, be confident that there is always milk coming.

Diagram of the breast:

Lobule

Lactiferous Duct

Ampulla (Lactiferous sinus)

Nipple

Lactiferous Tubule

Areola

Skin

Subcutaneous fat

Fibrous septum separating lobes

Lobes

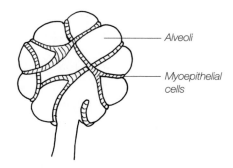

The Alveoli surrounded by myoepithelial cells
which propel the milk out of the lobule:

Breast

The breast is a secreting gland and is made up of approximately 20 lobes. Each lobe is divided into lobules which look like cauliflowers and consists of alveoli and ducts. Inside the alveoli are acini cells and it is these that produce the milk. Each Alveoli is surrounded by myoepithelial cells; these contract to propel or squeeze the milk into the ducts towards the nipple where it collects in the ampulla just under the areola, - the brown part surrounding your nipple. It is then expelled through the lactiferous tubules in the nipple and into your baby's mouth. The acini cells are constantly making more milk.

When your baby sucks at the breast, messages are sent along the nerve pathways to the brain. The pituitary gland in the brain produces hormones called prolactin and oxytocin. The hormone prolactin stimulates the acini cells to produce milk.

The hormone oxytocin (which is the same hormone which produces contractions of the uterus in labour) stimulates the myoepithelial cells around the Alveoli to contract and squeeze the milk towards the nipple where it flows out of the nipple to your baby.

Oxytocin is the 'feel good' hormone and for the letdown reflex to happen you need to be relaxed. I have seen women with full to bursting breast and the milk just won't come out. The baby is shouting at the breast and mum is worried she has no milk. Even when trying to express it just won't come out. I describe this scenario as when your bladder is full to bursting. Imagine you have been travelling for hours and you are bursting for a wee, you can't hold it any longer. You stop the car, there are no toilets, you are in the middle of nowhere, and you think – 'GREAT! I have got to go!' You get out of the car try to find somewhere and there is nowhere private. You know the passing traffic can see you but still you think, 'I really have to go'. So you prepare yourself and, low and behold, it won't come out - you cannot wee. You are too anxious and your body won't let it out because the muscles that hold it in won't relax.

For the breast to let out the milk you need to be relaxed too and not anxious. The oxytocin kicks in when baby starts to suck and the muscles contract around the cells to allow the milk to flow down. So never think you don't have milk there; you almost certainly do, but you need to believe it will flow, so relax and let it out.

Of course you may find breast feeding really easy and have no problems and your milk will just flow anyway so you will wonder what I am talking about.

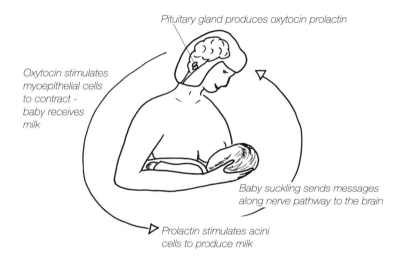

Pituitary gland produces oxytocin prolactin

Oxytocin stimulates myoepithelial cells to contract - baby receives milk

Baby suckling sends messages along nerve pathway to the brain

Prolactin stimulates acini cells to produce milk

Diagram of the let-down reflex suckling baby's messages to brain

Positioning baby on the breast

Get yourself comfortable. Grab a glass of water, the remote, your phone, magazines, whatever you might need as this can sometimes take an hour or more in the early days. It does get easier and baby gets more efficient at sucking, and your milk will flow more freely as the weeks go by, but at the beginning it can be lengthy so be patient and enjoy this time; it doesn't last forever.

If you are about to feed on your left breast then use your right hand to hold your baby across your body with your baby facing the left breast, with the left hand place your thumb at the top of the left breast and fingers underneath. This helps shape the breast so it is easier for your baby to latch on. Holding your baby at the shoulders, bring him towards the breast. As his mouth opens, bring your baby closer to latch onto the breast. Once he is sucking and is 'on' correctly and comfortable, you can relax both arms and shoulders. If you have very large breasts you may need to continue to hold the breast, as when you loosen it, it will drop and pull away from baby's mouth.

You know your baby is 'on' correctly as you will hear him sucking and swallowing. It should not hurt but may feel a little odd at first and your nipples should not be damaged i.e. cracked or sore. If they are damaged and cracked and sore you need to get more of the breast into the baby's mouth so the nipple is right at the back of the mouth where it is soft and not being squashed by the hard gums. Your baby will probably fall asleep at least ten minutes into the feed; this is where I recommend you burp your baby, then change the nappy and he will be awake again and will feed some more. You know your baby has fed well because he will then sleep for at least an hour after the feed. As the weeks pass, your baby will take more milk and should then manage to wake hungry at three hours from the start of the feed.

Diagrams of positioning

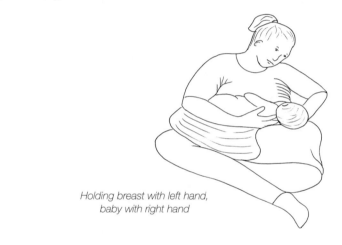

*Holding breast with left hand,
baby with right hand*

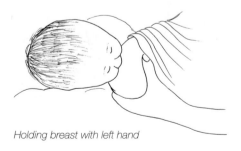

Holding breast with left hand

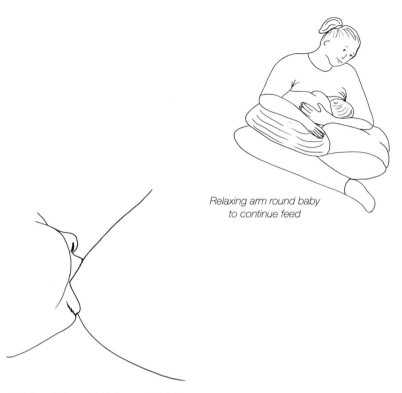

*Relaxing arm round baby
to continue feed*

Mouth onto breast with lips curled out

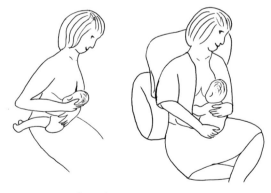

Other feeding positions to try

When feeding your baby think of it as supply and demand. The more your baby feeds, the more milk your breast will make for your baby. In the early days your baby grows rapidly so the appetite increases constantly. There will be days when he is feeding more frequently or for longer but don't worry he is just making more milk, and he will settle down again when his appetite is satisfied. Some babies will feed more frequently for just 24 hours, others for longer, maybe 48 hours but just let your baby feed. He is doing a good job at making more milk.

When your baby has been feeding you may notice that the inside of his lips go white and sometimes a little blister appears on the top lip. This is completely normal and is from the friction and the good suck of your baby.

Increasing milk supply with expressing

There may be a particular time of day where you think your breast milk may be low. If your baby is typically not settling from the 7pm feed and seems hungry, you can express after this feed for 2 days and your milk supply will increase and your baby should start to settle again. The same goes for any other time of day. Or you could express after every feed for 2 days to increase your supply.

Bottle feeding with expressed breast milk

If you are expressing because you are giving the expressed milk in a bottle - for example, you are not comfortable with breast feeding but you like the idea that your baby is having breast milk, or you can't breast feed because it is too uncomfortable or your baby doesn't suck well for whatever reason - then you should try to mimic the way a baby would naturally feed.

A breast-fed baby would naturally feed anywhere between two and half to four hourly feeds with little breaks whilst feeding, and would take a small amount of milk at one feed and large amount at another. So if you decide to express for say 15 minutes on each breast every 3 hours and stick to this rigidly, then your milk supply will not naturally increase.

So for your milk supply to continuously increase you need to express a little bit randomly and not in a rigid routine. So you could express 5 to 6 times a day, for example 7am then 10am which is 3 hours, then at 1.30pm, which is 3½ hours, then 4.30pm, which is back to 3 hours, again between 7.30pm and 8pm which is 3 to 3½ hours, then at 10.30pm. The next day you could allow a four hour gap between one feed and do a 2½ hour somewhere else, also, vary the length of time you express so you could do 20 minutes on both breasts then the next one 40 minutes on both breasts, then 15 minutes on both breasts etc.

Take a little break of say 10 minutes when expressing because you would probably change your babies nappy in the middle of a feed; also your milk will start to slow down and by taking a little break and going back to the same breast will often allow some more milk to start flowing.

Keep a record of times, how long you expressed and how much milk you expressed, and try to get a little bit more each day because your baby's appetite will be increasing all the time as he grows.

Example: Expressing log

Time	How long	How much	
7am	30mins left 30mins right	40mls 40mls	
11am	20mins left 20mins right	30mls 30mls	
3pm	25mins left 25mins right	40mls 40mls	
6pm	15mins left 15mins right	25mls 25mls	
10pm	30mins left 30mins right	40mls 40mls	
These times are just a guide; use them as an approximate guide	Adjust the duration slightly each day	Increase the amount every day	Eat well and drink well; rest when you can

Take a short break when expressing or switch breast then switch back.

These amounts are estimates only; your baby may start off drinking tiny amounts e.g. 60 – 90mls, but by the time your baby is 2 weeks old he may be drinking 100mls at each feed. At 3 to 4 weeks, 110mls to 120mls per feed. If you are giving expressed milk in a bottle and your baby is drinking it all, then increase it by 10mls, and keep increasing it each time they finish the new amount.

In my experience, and from seeing the amounts babies are drinking when giving expressed milk, they usually drink more in quantity than a formula-fed baby. So if you are looking at a formula guide, I would give at least 20 to 30mls more when giving breast milk. Only express during daytime hours; don't get yourself tired by expressing during the night. You should be sleeping when baby is sleeping.

Storage of milk

Once milk has been expressed it would keep well if left out of the fridge for a while because it has natural antibodies in the milk, but ideally put your milk straight into the fridge and store for 24 hours; if not used, put it in the freezer for later use. Try to use the milk as soon as possible, as the properties in it keep changing to meet your baby's nutritional requirements. Try to use within three months from freezer.

Breast feeding problems

Hopefully you are enjoying breast feeding your baby, but it doesn't always come without some problems. Here are a few that you might experience:

Engorgement

When you first start feeding, your breasts may become very full, hard and uncomfortable but they will settle down. Your baby has probably been feeding a lot and it has caused your breasts to make more milk than is needed. Once your baby settles into a feeding pattern of 2 to 3 hourly, your breasts will soften and settle down.

To ease discomfort you could hand-express a tiny bit of milk off your breast, just to make yourself comfortable. If you express too much with a pump, you will make the problem worse because you will be telling your breasts to produce more and more milk. If your breasts are too full the baby will find it hard to latch on, so if you hand-express a tiny bit to soften around the areola, your baby will be able to get on.

You can try putting hot or cold flannels on too. This can be comforting. There is also the old fashioned remedy of cabbage leaves from the fridge, - crush the stalks to release the juice (they don't smell very nice but it does ease the pain).

Continue to feed, it will ease off.

Sore nipples

If you baby is not properly latched on to your breast then there will be lots of friction on your nipples. They will be cracked and sore and may even bleed. This can also cause engorgement because your baby isn't emptying your breast properly.

Make sure your baby is latched onto the breast, not the nipple. Your baby's mouth should open wide and be well onto the breast so the nipple goes right to the back of baby's mouth; it should not be painful if baby is on properly. Your baby's lips should be curled out. (see picture previously)

If you are sore, use lots of moisturising cream after every feed. If it is too painful you can try nipple shields. These will give your nipples a rest. Try them for 48 hours and you should be able to go back to feeding without them.

If you have been feeding with no nipple problems and then develop sore pink nipples with a burning pain after feeding, this may be a sign of thrush, a fungal infection. Get this checked by your midwife or GP. You may need anti-fungal medication. If you have thrush on your breast you may have transferred it to your baby, so check inside your baby's mouth for white patches on the inside of cheeks and the edge of the tongue. Obviously the tongue will be white from milk, so marks on the cheeks could be more of an indication. Also the other way round - if your baby has oral thrush then he may have transferred it to your breast.

Flat nipples or inverted nipples

You can still feed your baby with flat or inverted nipples although it may be a little difficult to get baby on. Try pulling your nipple out and squeezing a little milk for baby to try to latch on to. If you are finding it really difficult, again nipple shields work well. Once baby is on and has pulled your nipple out, slip the shield off and latch baby on again or if it's easier, continue with the shield. I have seen women who have tried them as a temporary measure and continued to feed baby with them just fine. If it works for you, use it.

If it seems impossible to get your baby on and you want your baby to have breast milk, you can always express it and give it in the bottle.

Mastitis

Mastitis is a blocked milk duct caused when the milk has not been draining efficiently and has become stationary in a duct.

You will almost certainly know if you have mastitis as you will probably feel unwell. If you have a headache or fever, above 38°C or both, along with a hot red patch on your breast, then you should see your GP. For mastitis you may need antibiotics. It is very important that you continue to feed your baby; you must continue to drain the breast or it could turn to a more serious blockage of the duct and become a very painful abscess and need to be drained. Wear a good fitting bra as pressure from your bra can cause a blockage.

Try massaging your breast with the palm of your hand working from the chest towards the nipple to try to unblock the duct and get your milk flowing. You can do this whilst your baby is feeding. It will be uncomfortable, but persevere. You can also try warm flannels for comfort. You will be able to continue feeding.

Bottle feeding with formula

In the first few days after birth, even if you have chosen to bottle feed, your breast will start to produce milk and you will need to wear a good supporting bra. The breasts will become very full and may feel quite uncomfortable at approximately 3 days post-birth. This is called engorgement. Also you may find that you are very tearful as days 3 to 4 post-birth are typically what we call 'the baby blues'. This will not last long, maybe a day or two. You may feel you are crying for no reason – this is completely normal. If you haven't put your baby to the breast, your body will start to adjust itself and your breast will be returning to their pre-pregnancy, pre-birth size.

To bottle feed you will need at least six bottles, so let's look at the routine:-

First wash your hands.

Wash bottles with warm soapy water and rinse well. Sterilise, using your chosen equipment e.g. steam steriliser, microwave steriliser or cold water steriliser. You will need to sterilise the bottles every 24 hours. If you have used them or think they have been touched or contaminated in anyway e.g. you dropped it and the teat touched the floor, then you will need to re-sterilise.

It is important to sterilise your baby's bottles so there are no bacteria on them which your baby could ingest which could then cause an upset stomach, vomiting or diarrhoea. Vomiting and diarrhoea is far more serious in a baby than for an adult, as babies can become dehydrated very quickly and will need to be admitted to hospital because they have become seriously sick, so wash your hands and keep baby's feeding equipment clean and sterile.

When preparing the feed use freshly boiled water (allow it to cool for approximately 10 minutes so it is not scalding); measure the correct amount of cooled boiled water into the bottle. Be very careful as water is still hot. Add the required amounts of powder, usually 1 ounce of water to 1 ounce of powder (1 scoop). Screw the teat on and place the top on; cool to the required temperature for your baby. Place the bottle into a jug of cold water to cool it.

Follow the guidelines on the formula container. It will tell you not only how much to give, depending on the age of your baby, but also by the weight of your baby, so make adjustments if your baby is lighter than average or heavier than average.

Once you have made up the feed I would suggest you throw away any that is left after an hour, as milk at room temperature or warmed up has an increased risk of growing bacteria and causing an upset stomach.

If you are timing baby's feeds, then the time he starts his feed is the time you use, so if baby is on a 3-hourly routine, he would be hungry approximately 3 hours after he started the feed. Also try to get your baby to finish the feed within the hour otherwise if he drinks it after an hour of starting the feed he probably won't be hungry at 3 hours from start, as the little feed he had late will stop him from being hungry, and then by the end of the day you won't know what he has had to eat and could possibly be a whole feed down by the time you go to bed. Your baby will then wake up hungry in the night.

Combination feeding

As a Maternity Nurse I usually do the late evening feed and the night feeds. Some mums choose to express in the mornings so I have milk to give the baby and she can go to bed early and rest. Some mums say to me at the start, "I am only breast feeding from 7am to 7pm," so then I give formula for the other feeds. There is no reason why you can't do the same if you are finding solely breast feeding difficult. The baby doesn't get confused if he has a bottle then breast, in fact the earlier you give a bottle the better because they don't get confused. Your body will adjust to how many feeds you are doing and your milk will still continue to increase in the daytime and you will be well rested.

Obviously, if breast feeding is working for you then you will be finding it easy to feed in the night and drop off back to sleep, but if you are exhausted and thinking of giving up then try this combination feeding option. You will find you can continue for quite some time and your baby will soon give up the evening and night time feeds, so he can continue on the breast in the daytime until weaning.

I have never had a newborn baby (under one month old) with nipple confusion; they instinctively know how to suck a bottle and how to milk the breast. If you exclusively feed your baby only from the breast for a month then your baby will not take a bottle easily, because he will have become used to the breast. The way a baby sucks from a bottle is very different from the breast, so introduce an expressed milk feed early to prevent a problem. Again if you intend to breast feed for a long time then your baby will never need a bottle so can go straight to a cup.

The First Two Weeks

Your baby changes every day

For the first six weeks, expect things to change. Just when you think you have everything under control, you have had the perfect routine for days and then it all seems to go wrong. Don't worry it hasn't! Your baby is probably hungry, or is just tired today. He is a little human being after all and won't function like a robot, so just go with the flow, it doesn't matter if you have to move feeds a little because you have an appointment or need to be somewhere. Just adjust your day as you go. As long as he has eaten well between 6/7am and 11pm then he should only need to feed once in the night.

Don't expect too much of your little one. You will have some sleepless nights for these first six weeks, but when you look at the big picture, six weeks out of your life is a very short time and this time with your baby is so precious because it goes by so fast and he will be changing in looks, gaining weight, and making little happy noises. So enjoy.

Typical days, week by week

I have set out a typical day as a guide to follow week by week and you will notice that each week there are little changes. This is because the first two weeks your baby pretty much eats and sleeps, but by week three your baby is awake much more, then by week six, a routine is set which can stay in place for some time and you only need to cut back on the nap times.

Day 1 – colostrum – breast feeding

When your baby is born he will probably breast feed within the first hour of life. At this stage your breast contains colostrum; a thick yellowish liquid that contains all the nutrients of fats, sugars, vitamins and minerals, antibodies and proteins that your baby needs for the first three to four days. This first milk coats the lining of the stomach and intestine, protecting it from pathogens sticking to it; it also helps the gut to continue to mature. Your baby only needs a tiny amount to keep energy levels up and their little stomachs can only hold small amounts, so little and often is the key. All babies are different some will have a little 5 minute feed on each breast and sleep for hours and others will feed on and off every hour for hours. This is normal, let them feed as often as they like.

Each day your breast will start to produce more milk. Baby will want to feed for a little longer at the breast and will then sleep for a little longer between feeds, maybe 2 hours or, if you are lucky, 3 to 4 hours. Some babies feed very little and sleep a lot in these early days and others want to feed constantly.

By day 3 to 4, your post-birth milk will probably be in. You will know it's there because your breast will feel quite full. Your baby will probably feed for approximately 15 to 20 minutes on each breast and you will hear him swallowing the milk when feeding. Others may feed for less time and some will feed for longer, up to 1 hour or more, at the breast. Let him feed as little or as often as he likes for these early days.

First two weeks breast feeding

By the end of the first week your milk supply should be increasing every day and hopefully so will your confidence to feed your baby. The length of time your baby needs to feed is very individual and you will find what works for you. You need to feed for long enough that your baby settles and doesn't feed again for at least 3 hours from the start of that feed. Some babies will feed quickly, 15-20 minutes on one breast and be satisfied and others will feed up to 30 minutes on both breasts or a little longer. You will realize baby is taking enough when he falls asleep and stays asleep for several hours before demanding more.

As a maternity nurse I advise mothers to let the baby feed for as long as he likes (they normally fall asleep at the breast), then burp them, if needed, and change the nappy. This shifts any wind and wakes them up. He can then be offered the same breast if he hasn't fed for long, let's say less than 20 minutes, or the other breast and he will feed some more and settle to sleep for longer.

To get your baby to sleep well, he needs to eat well. If you have fed your baby and he seems settled then wakes and is hungry after an hour, feed for longer next time and wake him up whilst feeding. Make sure baby is feeding and swallowing and not just snoozing at the breast.

Some babies will feed for just a short time at the breast and sleep and feed four hourly. Others will feed for over an hour and still need to feed two and a half to three hourly; they are all different and it is all normal.

If your baby seems to be feeding a lot, don't worry, he is only a week old and will get more efficient at feeding. As a baby grows their tummy grows too and can take bigger feeds and it does get easier.

By week two your baby will have fallen into a pattern of three hourly feeding, if feeding well.

It is quite common for some babies to feed a lot in the evenings. Again don't worry, he is just stimulating the breast to produce more milk; this will settle down.

In my experience most babies want to just eat and sleep for the first two weeks. Enjoy this time for lots of cuddles and for you to rest when your baby is sleeping.

Two steps forwards one step back

You may be two and a half to three weeks in and your baby seems to be following his own routine of three hourly feeds, when suddenly it seems like it's all going wrong. Your baby is crying and hungry all the time. This is perfectly normal when breast feeding.

Some babies want to feed a lot in the evenings or some just more frequently all day; some keep to a similar time but feed for longer. Because breast feeding is supply and demand, your baby has to make more milk by suckling at the breast. He is growing very fast, gaining approximately 1oz/30g per day, so their appetite is increasing too. Your milk supply has to increase to satisfy the demand. The only way to do this is for more milk to be taken off the breast so feed whenever it is needed. This increase in appetite usually lasts for approximately 2 days and everything calms back to normal. Just let your baby do the job of making more milk, even if it feels like you can't possibly have any left in there.

He will then go back to his little routine, possibly for four or five days, then an increase in demand will return again, which is why it feels like two steps forward and one step back, but slowly you will get there.

Babies grow rapidly in the first months and all babies are different, but at three weeks and six weeks these growth spurts are very noticeable so bear with it. The increase in demand for milk only lasts a couple of days.

Bottle feeding - day one

Your baby has just been born and is quite alert and will probably look around for a little while meeting his mummy and daddy. You will probably be encouraged by the Midwife to feed your baby within the hour of birth.

You will choose a formula to give your baby - it may be a small choice at the hospital or you might give what your friends or family have already used with their babies.

To bottle feed your baby, make yourself comfortable it could take 5 minutes for your baby to drain the bottle or it may take an hour. Some babies will 'guzzle' it down really quickly, burp, and they are done; others will slowly feed, slowly burp, then need a 20 minute rest before finishing the rest.

Sit comfortably, hold your baby cradled in your arms with their head slightly higher than their body. Offer the teat to your baby; if he is hungry he will root towards the teat. This is a natural rooting reflex where the baby will open his mouth and try to latch on to the teat. Put the teat in baby's mouth and hold the bottle upside down so the milk drains towards the teat making sure that the teat is full of milk all the time so baby is not sucking air as this will cause wind. Let your baby feed and suck for as long as he likes, he might finish the bottle in one go or more likely stop halfway through. You then need to sit baby upright so he can burp freely or put him on your shoulder to burp.

For your baby's very first feed, I would only allow him to drink a small amount - 30 to 40mls, as the stomach is so tiny. This is sufficient to keep his blood sugar levels up, after the long exhausting journey of birth.

If you allow your baby to drink a full feed of 90mls it is likely that your baby will vomit most of it back because the stomach is so small and needs to stretch as he grows.

After this feed your baby may sleep anything from 2 to maybe 5 hours. I would wake baby and give him a feed if he is sleeping past 4 to 5 hours, as babies blood sugars can drop if they go a long time without food in the first 24 hours.

In the first 24 hours your baby uses a lot of energy coping with the stress of birth, and adjusting to the cooler temperature of the outside world. You may think it is nice and warm at a room temperature of 22 to 24 degrees Celsius, but your baby was in an environment of 37 degrees Celsius - as warm as the Caribbean - so it will feel cold. Remember, as they came out wet they will lose more heat, so it is also important to have your baby dressed in a nappy, a vest, a sleep suit and, if very small, a hat too.

For the next feed, I would allow baby to take a little more milk, maybe 40 to 50mls. Increase each feed depending on what he is drinking e.g. if he takes 40mls at the first feed, I would expect him to drink the same at the next feed or a little drop more. If he then takes 50mls comfortably and keeps it down, I would subsequently offer 60mls at the next feed.

The first 24 hours your baby can be very sleepy after the first feed but, by day 2, your baby will probably want to feed 2 to 3 hourly but may sleep up to 4 hours. I would wake baby at four hours to feed so that he doesn't wake in the night for 3 hourly feeding.

By the end of baby's second week I would expect him to be drinking 3oz, 90mls of formula at every feed and feeding as often as three to four hours, and only waking once in the night at approximately 2.30 to 3am.

Age	Number of feeds per 24 hours	How much for each feed
Birth to 2 weeks	6 to 8	Up to 90ml/ 3oz
2 to 4 weeks	5 to 6	Up to 120ml/4oz
4 to 8 weeks	5 to 6	Up to 150ml/5oz
8 to 12 weeks	5	Up to 180ml/6oz

This is an approximate guide as your baby may drink more or less in quantity and may drink more or fewer bottles per day depending on weight. Your baby will start with a 2 to 3-hourly schedule then progress to a 3½-hourly schedule then possibly to 4-hourly.

Daily Routines Week by Week

Routines

Typical day for a one week old - (adjust the time you start your day, depending what happened in the night, and then continue three-hourly feeding. Some babies may still want to feed a bit more often than this, so anywhere between 2 and 3 hours.) I advise changing the nappy halfway through to wake baby but a bottle fed baby will stop when he is ready and may not be as sleepy as a breast fed baby.

6.30am

Feed, half way through, change nappy. Give the rest of the feed. Burp, then swaddle and place back in basket to sleep. This would probably take up to an hour

Go back to sleep if you can.

9.30am

Feed, half way through, wash your baby's face to freshen up and change nappy, then give the rest of the feed, burp and swaddle and place back in basket to sleep or just cuddle and enjoy your baby.

12.30pm

Feed, then change half way through, then give the rest of the feed. Burp and swaddle to sleep. Continue this sequence all day.

3.30pm

Feed and change

6.30pm

Feed and change

9.30pm

Feed, or if your baby is sleeping I would leave him until 10.30pm but no longer than four hours. You want the longest sleep whilst you are sleeping. Swaddle and settle for bed, and fingers crossed, you get four hours or more sleep.

If your baby is full-term and healthy, and has no medical issues, let him wake you. He will probably wake at approximately 1.30/2am, then 5.30/6am-ish.

A typical day for a 2 week old - (again adjust the start time depending on what night you had):

7.00am

Feed, change half way through, then feed. Burp, swaddle and settle.

You sleep if you can.

10.00am

Feed, change, finish feed. Burp, swaddle and settle (or your baby might be awake and want to look around for 10 minutes, then settle to sleep).

1.00pm

Feed, change, finish feed. Burp, swaddle and settle (or your baby might be awake and want to look around for 10 minutes, then settle to sleep).

4.00pm

Feed, then half way through, give a bath, (look at section on bath time). Then finish feed and swaddle and settle in basket. Your baby will be very tired.

7.00pm

Leave until 7.30pm if sleeping and wake for feed. Change, burp and finish feed, swaddle and settle in basket.

10.30pm

Feed, change, feed and straight back to sleep.

Now you go to bed too and hope for some sleep. Let your baby wake you.

Hopefully your baby will let you sleep until 2.30am if you're lucky. Feed, change, finish feed and burp. Settle to sleep.

Then 6 to 6.30am start your new day.

Week three:

Your baby is uncurling and becoming more awake and getting louder. He will be awake for the feed then will stay awake for a little while. I think 1½ hours is plenty long enough for your baby to be awake and will show signs of wanting to go to sleep. If your baby has been awake over an hour and is yawning or getting grumpy then it's time to wrap them up and put them in their basket.

When baby is awake he might like to watch a mobile, or lie on a baby gym, or just sit in his chair and look around.

A guide to try at three weeks:

Feed times - these are the times you start the feed:

7 30am, 10.30am, 1.30pm, 4.30pm, 7.30pm, 10.30pm.

This is three hourly. Adjust the time to suit you. You may want to start at 7 or 8am.

Once your baby has fed, let him look around for a little while depending on how long he has been awake. Then put him back in his basket awake so he will learn to self-settle.

You don't have to get up at this early time of the day; you and your baby can always go back to bed after the morning feed and get a bit more sleep.

Another option for a three week old:

7am
Feed, change, finish feed and let your baby stay awake, looking around under a mobile or baby gym. Your baby should not be awake longer than an hour and a half from start of feed. He will get very tired.

8.30am
Swaddle and settle back to sleep.

10.00am
Feed, change, finish feed, burp, and let your baby stay awake for a while.

11.30am
Swaddle, burp and settle to sleep.

1.00pm
Feed, stay awake no longer than an hour and a half.

2.30pm
Swaddle, settle and sleep

4.00pm
Feed, stay awake.

5.30 pm
Burp, swaddle and settle to sleep for 45 minutes. This is a power nap just to get them through to bath and bedtime.

6.45pm

Wake baby, give a bath and massage then feed, burp, finish feed and settle straight to sleep.

10.30pm

Feed, change, finish feed, burp, swaddle, and straight back to sleep. All to bed and fingers crossed for some sleep.

Hopefully, wake at approximately 2.30 to 3am, feed and settle straight back to sleep. Then get through to 7am - fingers crossed.

Alternative week 3:

If your baby is showing signs of tiredness e.g. yawning or crying, put him to sleep before the times mentioned.

7am

Feed, change, finish feed then let your baby stay awake looking around under a mobile or baby gym. Your baby should be awake no longer than an hour and a half from start of feed. He will get very tired.

8.30am

Swaddle and settle back to sleep. Some babies may take a while to fall asleep but should be asleep by 9am at latest or they will get over tired.

10.30am

If you are always waking your baby for this feed at 10am, you could try 10.30am (so, 3½ hours from last feed). Feed, change, finish feed, burp and let your baby stay awake for a while.

12 noon

Swaddle, burp and settle to sleep.

2.30pm (so 4 hours from last feed)

Feed, stay awake no longer than an hour and a half.

4.00pm

Swaddle, settle and sleep.

5.00pm (2½ hours from last feed)

Small feed, stay awake.

5.45pm

Play, gym or chair.

6.45pm (1½ hours from last feed - stock up for bedtime)

Bath and massage, then feed, burp, finish feed and settle straight to sleep.

i.e. baby will have had more than one full feed but less than two.

10.00pm

Feed, change, finish feed, burp, swaddle and straight back to sleep. All to bed and fingers crossed for some sleep. Only change nappy if it has poo in it.

Hopefully wake at approximately 2.30 to 3.00am, feed and settle straight back to sleep. Then get through to 7am.

Week four:

At this stage I start to get a little bit strict about waking times. Your baby should be able to be awake for about an hour and a half to one hour 45mins at each waking time. I also adjust the feed times. However it is trial and error, so if it doesn't work and your baby wakes up in the evening or is awake in the night, then go back to three hourly.

A typical day for a four week old - (again, adjust your start time and work around it to fit in appointments):

7.00 am

Feed as usual, burp, nappy change, give rest of feed, then on play gym. Your baby should be ready to sleep after an hour and a half of being awake.

8.30am

Settle to sleep. Baby should sleep for an hour and a half.

10.00am

Feed as usual, burp, nappy change, give rest of feed then on play gym.

11.30am

Settle to bed in the quiet. If your baby is happy and satisfied with food he will lie happily looking around then fall asleep. If baby has been lying happily, then you know he is not hungry. He may start to cry a little when tired but just leave him and he will go to sleep. Hopefully he will sleep for 2 hours. If baby can manage 2 hours then feed at 2.00pm, but feed anywhere between 1.00 and 2.00pm.

2.00pm

Feed as usual, burp, nappy change, give rest of feed, then on play gym or chair, or just a chat with you or friends.

3.30pm

Settle to sleep. Baby should sleep for an hour and a half.

5.00pm

Feed on breast or half a bottle and burp – give a small feed.

6.00pm

Give a nice relaxing bath followed by a massage.

6.30pm

Give other breast or rest of the bottle then settle to sleep.

7.00pm

Asleep in bed for the evening.

10.00pm

Give a very sleepy feed, try not to disturb baby too much. Lift baby from the cot, arouse him just enough to get him to feed. Let him feed for as long as possible, burp him gently and place him back to sleep. Only change the nappy if it has a poo in it.

Then off to bed and hope he sleeps past 2/2.30am. Your baby will probably be managing four or five hours from 10.00pm by now but don't worry if not, it will come.

A typical day for a 5 week old:

Your baby should be able to stay awake for 2 hours now so try and get him to do one four hour session from 10.00 to 2.00 or 10.30 to 2.30.

Baby now needs to eat approximately 120ml to 150ml per feed, depending on weight (this is for a 10lb baby).

7.00am

Feed as usual, burp, nappy change, give rest of feed then on play gym or chair. Your baby should be ready to sleep after 2 hours; try and keep him awake. This will make a difference to his night time sleeping.

9.00 - 10.00am

Sleep for one hour. Your baby will probably wake after half an hour but if he is sleeping wake up at 10.00.

10.30am

Feed - this is stretching to three and half hours. Then awake time. Gym chair or under mobile.

12.00 - 2.30pm

Sleep - Baby should sleep well here, up to two and half hours. If he hasn't woken, wake at 2.30.

2.30pm

Feed, burp, change, waking time etc. Try and keep your baby awake until 4.30pm.

4.30pm to 5.30pm

Sleep.

5.30pm

Awake. Gym or naked time in bathroom on mat on the floor.

6.00pm

Bath and massage followed by a feed.

Keep awake whilst feeding, burp well then in to bed for 7.00pm.

10.00pm

Lift for sleepy feed. Then fingers crossed for a good night.

A typical day for a six week old:

Your baby should be awake for 2 hours at a time now. You are now trying to stretch your baby's feeds to three and half to four hours. The baby may manage three and a half in the morning then four hours over lunch, then three to three and a half in the afternoon until six-thirty. Continue this routine for a month or longer, it depends if your baby is ready. By ten to twelve weeks your baby should manage a four hour routine, but he must be fed well, awake and alert at play times and sleep well.

If you have a routine that is working and your baby is sleeping well at night then don't change it.

7.00am
Feed as usual, burp, nappy change, give rest of feed then on play gym or chair. Your baby should be ready to sleep after 2 hours. Try and keep them awake; this will make a difference to their night time sleeping.

9.00 - 10.00am
Sleep for one hour; your baby will probably wake after half an hour but if he is sleeping, wake him up at 10.00am.

10.30 - 11am
Feed - this is now stretching to four hours. Then awake time. (Gym chair under mobile). Only do this if baby is able to. Obviously if he is crying and can't be consoled with playing or distraction then feed at 10.30.

12.00 - 2.30pm
Sleep. Baby should sleep well here, up to two and half hours. If he hasn't woken, wake at 2.30.

2.30 - 3.00pm
Depending if baby fed at 10.30 or 11.00am, feed, burp, change, awake time etc. Try and keep him awake until 4.30pm.

4.30pm Sleep for half an hour (longer if needed).

5.00 - 5.30pm
Awake. Gym or naked time in bathroom on mat on the floor.

6.00pm
Bath and massage followed by a feed; burp well then in to bed for 7.00pm

10.00pm

Lift for sleepy feed. Then fingers crossed for a good night.

You can then follow this routine pretty much until weaning. You only need to cut back on nap times. By three months your baby should only need a 15-30min nap in the morning, 2 hours at lunch time and 15 minutes at 5-ish but if your baby is grumpy and needs more sleep then let him sleep a bit longer. Just make little adjustments and find what works.

Typical day for a ten to twelve week old, plus:

Your baby should manage a four hourly routine by now but don't worry if he hasn't got to this stage yet. Continue with the three and three and half hour routine with a four hour at midday. Again your baby may be starting his day at a different time, so adjust this to suit you.

7.00am

Feed, awake on gym or chair whilst you snooze in bed or get up and shower; give rest of feed as long as he feeds within the hour from when you started.

9.30-10.00am

Sleep. Wake him up. Half an hour should be long enough; it's just a power nap.

11.00am

Feed, awake playing, then give rest of feed.

12.30 - 2.30pm

Sleep. Some babies may not need this much sleep. If baby wakes try and let him go back to sleep.

3.00pm

Feed, then play or activity, give rest of feed.

4.30pm

Sleep fifteen minutes to half an hour maximum.

5.45pm

Bed time bath or massage.

Your baby probably won't want to wait until 7.00 for a feed, so feed any time after 6.00 then settle to bed.

10.00pm

If your baby is still doing the sleepy feed, then give this at 10.00-ish.

Hopefully your baby is sleeping through the night.

Common illnesses/occurrences

Jaundice

Jaundice is quite a common condition in the newborn baby. If your baby has arrived early, or is small, or has had a forceps or suction delivery, it is more likely that he will get jaundice.

If this happens 24 hours after birth, this is called physiological jaundice and is common. If this happens in the first 24 hours after birth, this is a more serious form of jaundice as is not physiological and will need medical attention.

Your baby's skin will be yellow, similar to a sun tan and the whites of the eyes will be yellow too.

The cause is your baby having more red blood cells in the blood than he needs. This can be from the surge of blood from the placenta to baby just as baby is born, before the cord is cut and clamped, or from bruising on the head or a haematoma, caused by suction or forceps, which is trauma to blood vessels under the skin. As the body breaks down these extra blood cells it produces bilirubin. This causes the skin and whites of the eyes to be yellow.

The only way for your baby to get rid of the bilirubin is for the liver to break it down then pass it to the gut, where it is expelled. When your baby opens its bowels, it comes out in the poo. Also it becomes water soluble and passes out with the urine. It will not cause any discomfort but your baby may be sleepy. So, it is IMPORTANT, to wake your baby and feed every 3 hours.

By feeding your baby frequently will allow the bilirubin to pass out of your baby into his nappy. Therefore you want your baby to poo and wee often. Also sunlight on your baby's skin is what makes it water soluble so it can pass out in the urine. Undress your baby in a warm room and place him in the natural day light, - not directly in the sun or your baby will burn.

If the midwife is concerned then she will prick your baby's heel to get a small amount of blood to be tested. Most of the time, feeding frequently and daylight are the only treatments needed but if your baby's bilirubin levels are raised beyond a normal level, then your baby may need to be re-admitted to hospital where he will be given ultraviolet light therapy. This involves your baby lying in just a nappy, lying under the light with his eyes covered to protect them. This action speeds up the bilirubin becoming water soluble and your baby can excrete it out in the urine. Once the bilirubin levels are falling your baby will be discharged and can go home.

If your baby is yellow and sleepy, has dark yellow urine and/or pale stools, tell your midwife or GP.

Cord care

You DO NOT need to do anything to the umbilical cord, just keep an eye on it. If it becomes red and sore or is excessively smelly, wet and oozing, tell your midwife or GP, otherwise leave it alone. It rots off naturally, so it will smell a little, and then drop off. Usually between 5 to 14 days but it may take longer if the cord is thick.

Cradle cap

This is very common and is the build-up of dead skin cells and oils from the skin and usually builds up around the eyebrows forehead and scalp. If it goes unnoticed, then it can become quite thick and crusty. It will continue in to the early years and some toddlers will continue to have it.

To prevent it, you can put baby oil or sunflower oil/olive oil etc. on your baby's head and forehead, leave it to soak for several hours then rub the skin with a muslin cloth gently but firmly. You will notice the dead skin coming off. It is like exfoliation. Then wash your baby's hair. This will keep it at bay if you do it often. If it has become thick and crusty, do not pick at it, as this can cause infection.

You can also buy shampoo to remove cradle cap and then continue to use it for prevention.

Sticky eyes

This is very common as babies tear ducts are so small the tears cannot drain away down the duct. It normally corrects itself as baby grows. As long as the white of the eye is white, not red, and is just sticky, this is nothing to worry about.

You can wash your baby's eyes by squirting breast milk into the eye or you can put some breast milk onto cotton wool and wipe your baby's eye from nose to ear. Breast milk is good as it is sterile, is warm and has antibodies in it which help healing. If you are not breast feeding you can use cooled boiled water.

If the eye is excessively sticky or oozing a yellow substance or is constantly wet and making the surrounding part of the eye sore, or the conjunctiva - the white part of the eye - is red then tell your midwife or GP.

Common Cold

Common cold symptoms with babies are the same symptoms as for an adult. For example, a headache, sore throat, runny nose, and raised temperature, but your baby cannot tell you this, He may not be his normal happy and settled self, or he may be crying a lot and seem quite irritable along with a raised temperature and a runny nose which you can of course see. You can give the recommend dose of paracetamol medicine for babies to ease the symptoms and if your baby seems to have a blocked nose full of mucus, you can use saline drops and vapour rub for the chest to help clear the nose. Check the age recommendations and always follow the instructions on any medications.

Temperature

If your baby is sleepy or irritable and seems unwell and feels a little hot, you may need to take their temperature. If it is more than 38°C, you can give children's paracetamol. **Give for the correct age.** You can buy for 2 months plus and 6 months plus. If the temperature does not come down after 40 minutes to an hour, but has not risen, you can keep an eye on your baby and give a second dose 4 hours later. Encourage your baby to drink to prevent dehydration.

Trust your instinct. If you are worried about your baby then contact your GP.

If your baby or child has a temperature of 40°C, - this is a very high temperature - and also has cold hands and feet, this can be a sign of serious infection. Seek medical help straight away. Your baby will probably be very lethargic or very agitated.

To take your baby's temperature you can use either a digital thermometer which you put in the ear. It is very quick and easy and beeps when the results are ready in seconds.

You can use a digital thermometer which you place under the arm, right into the arm pit then hold baby's arm down by his side. Wait for the beep and read results.

There are also infrared thermometers, where you don't even need to touch your baby's skin. You pass them in front of your baby's skin approximately 2-3 cm away and it beeps with a very quick and accurate reading.

DO NOT use a rectal thermometer. This can cause serious damage to your baby i.e. perforation of the rectum. These are rarely used these days with advanced technology of digital thermometers for the ear, armpit and skin.

Heat rash

Heat rash is probably the most common rash. It is little raised spots that pop up anywhere but typically around the back of the neck and shoulders. If your baby seems hot, then loosen the clothing and take off some layers.

Dribble rash

Dribble rash is a rash around the mouth and is caused from your baby constantly dribbling. When your baby is teething he will dribble a lot, so the skin around your baby's mouth is constantly wet with saliva. Try to keep the area dry by patting gently. You can put a gentle moisturising cream around the mouth when your baby goes to sleep to help healing.

Millia

These are tiny white or yellowish spots, also called milk spots, on the face, typically around and on the nose. These spots are caused from hormones passed from the mother to the baby.

Baby acne

Baby acne is also caused from the hormones passed from the mother to the baby and your baby's face may be very spotty and they could be anywhere on baby's face - from jaw line up to the cheeks or on the forehead. This will settle down and disappear after several weeks.

Constipation

Constipation is when your baby is finding it difficult to open his bowels and when they are open the poo is dry and hard like pellets. This can be uncomfortable and cause tummy ache and is also very uncomfortable when passing poo.

It is very unusual for a breast-fed baby to be constipated. If your baby does not have a bowel movement for several days whilst breast feeding, as long as when they do it is soft and normal, it is ok. Sometimes when a baby has a growth spurt, all of the food is utilised and stored as fat, so there is no waste. Once the growth spurt settles and food increases, bowel movements will be regular again, soft and normal.

Formula-fed babies can sometimes get constipated, especially if just changing from breast milk to formula or when the weather is hot and your baby may be thirsty.

Formula milk is much more slowly digested than breast milk, so when changing to this, your baby may be a little uncomfortable. It soon passes as your baby gets used to this. If the weather is really hot, your baby may need to drink water in between feeds, as he may be thirsty, not hungry.

If your baby is constipated, you can give cool boiled water which should help to keep the motion soft.

Diarrhoea

Diarrhoea is much looser than breast milk poo. It is very watery, may be slightly green and smell stronger and more offensive than a normal poo.

It can be caused by a viral infection, possibly a virus contracted from someone else or a bacterial infection where bacteria could be growing and your baby has ingested it. For example, if the bottles, teats or dummies/soothers have not been cleaned and sterilised correctly, or you have left warmed milk out of the fridge long enough for bacteria to grow i.e. more than 1-2 hours, then given it to your baby.

Newborn babies' tummies are very immature and need to build up immunity to bugs that they come into contact with, so for the first six to nine months it is best to keep everything that goes into your baby's mouth clean/sterile.

Continue to feed your baby as normal and give extra cooled boiled water, as your baby can become very dehydrated, which is dangerous. If you think your baby has diarrhoea then consult your GP.

Nail infection (Paronychia)

A paronychia is an inflammation which develops next to the finger nail and is quite common on babies' tiny finger nails. Sometimes it just appears for no real reason. The skin peels down the side of the nail and it looks a little red and sore.

It may appear if you have torn your babies nail off and it tears down the side of the finger, so do be careful when cutting/biting nails.

There is no need to do anything at this stage if they are just noticeable. Keep an eye on it and it should heal by itself. Continue with normal cleanliness, washing your hands regularly and cleaning baby's hands when in the bath.

If the finger becomes very swollen and/or oozes pus, then it has become infected and you will need to see your Midwife or GP.

Hiccups

Hiccups are completely normal. We as adults often get hiccups if we have eaten a big meal or drunk too quickly. A baby often gets them after feeding. If your baby has fed well and is contented but has hiccups, don't worry yourself about them, just settle baby to bed. He may continue to hiccup, they will subside and baby will fall asleep. If they seem to be bothering him, then lift baby and sit him upright for a few minutes until they pass, then settle him into bed again to sleep.

Thrush

Thrush infection is when an imbalance of the body's natural flora occurs. It is caused from Candida albicans. This is something that lives naturally in our body. Sometimes an imbalance occurs and the Candida albicans takes over, causing thrush.

If your baby has this infection, he will have white spots on the inside of the mouth, inside the cheeks or gums or tongue - not to be mistaken for milk stain. If your baby has just fed and the tongue is white this is normal but if it is on the insides of the mouth, the tip of the tongue and gums and cannot be wiped away, then this is thrush. It will be sore on your baby's mouth and your baby may find it difficult or uncomfortable to feed. He may pull off the breast or teat whilst feeding. It is common in babies and occurs because the baby may have low immunity, so it is just one of those things which happen.

It can be caused from dummies or soothers not being sterilised, so make sure you keep them clean and sterilise them daily. If you are breast feeding and you or your baby has been prescribed antibiotics for any reason, then this can kill some of the natural bacteria which we need to keep our natural flora in balance and this will often cause thrush.

If your baby has thrush and you are breast feeding then check your breast too as you can get thrush in your breast. Your nipples will be very pink and tender and you may have shooting pains into your breast when feeding.

If you suspect that you or your baby has thrush then see your GP. You may need medication.

Colic

Colic is a difficult one, because I believe it is a word used to describe an irritable or unsettled baby, whereas people today use it to define a condition.

Babies cry for lots of reasons; they could be hungry, and in the very early days the most crying is done because of hunger. It may seem like they have only just fed, but they are ready for some more.

Wind can be uncomfortable and for some babies very painful, so it's important to get wind up before baby falls asleep or wind gets trapped and is more difficult to shift. The word wind itself is sometimes called colic and if that is the case, all babies have colic, because we know that they all need burping to bring up the wind.

Tiredness is a reason for crying and this is the most difficult for parents to deal with because they have fed the baby, he has burped well, had a little chat with mum, dad, grandparents etc., and is now ready to be put down in his cot to settle to sleep. Baby lies there for a few minutes then starts crying. So of course he is picked up. If baby is only crying because he is tired and he is constantly picked up, he can't go off to sleep. Some babies need to be left to cry themselves to sleep.

Some babies will lie happily in their cot looking around and cooing, and drop off to sleep. Others will look around for a few minutes, and start crying. Some will turn it into a scream and just stop suddenly to sleep. This crying confuses parents. They think something is wrong, when most of the time the baby is saying 'I am really tired and I can't get to sleep'. If your baby is crying and throwing arms in the air or punching the air or just jerking his arms about, then I would swaddle the baby and put him back in his cot and he will cry to sleep. If he is an older baby, over 6 weeks, then your baby may be so tired and over stimulated that he can't go to sleep, so will need to be put somewhere quiet, as any noise will jerk him awake or be irritating your baby. An over-stimulated baby will scream and it is natural to think they are in pain when they may just be very tired.

Like ourselves, if you are relaxed and go to bed you generally sleep well and will drop off easily to sleep, but if you are tired or stressed about something your mind can't shut off. You become more irritable and more tired and can't get to sleep. You need to have silence because anything irritates you. Babies are the same.

Some babies may need to be swaddled and then calmed in your arms for a few minutes, but I always like to put baby in the cot, slightly awake so baby knows where he is. If you let him fall asleep on you, then place him in the cot he is going to wake up wondering where he is and how he got there. Baby was in a soft warm place all cuddled up, close to someone, and now they are gone, so it is natural baby will cry. Settle baby in your arms by all means, and when he is looking dozy but not asleep, put him in his cot. That way baby will go off to sleep and sleep well, knowing where he is.

Obviously if you think your baby cries excessively or doesn't eat well and is not gaining weight or brings their knees up and seems to be in pain, there could be a medical problem e.g reflux, silent reflux, lactose intolerance or something else, so consult your GP.

Reflux

Some reflux, as in spitting back milk, can be normal. This is called a posset. Some babies will burp and bring back what seems quite a lot of milk; this is normal too. The valve or muscle which closes the stomach, between the oesophagus and the stomach, is weak in newborn babies and if they eat excessively, which they mostly do, and the stomach is full, the valve will open and the milk will spill back out of the stomach, up the oesophagus and out through the mouth. This can be quite alarming if it is a lot of milk, but if your baby is happy and is gaining weight, then it is probably nothing to worry about. Obviously mention this to your GP if you are worried.

If your baby is vomiting at most feeds and it is projectile vomiting, is crying excessively and cannot be put down flat in his cot because milk spills up and out of the mouth or nose, this is reflux and there may be an underlying cause. See your GP.

Silent Reflux

If your baby struggles to feed, only takes small amounts, cries excessively, screams a lot and arches his back or straightens back, cannot be put down flat, is not gaining weight or is slow to gain weight, and is not vomiting or spilling back milk, then this is silent reflux.

Silent reflux is when the small drop of milk baby is able to eat stays in the stomach but the acid that is produced in the stomach to break down the milk spills back up the oesophagus. This burns the oesophagus and causes pain. Your baby will not be able to lie flat as the acid will spill back up.

For reflux and silent reflux you can raise the head end of your baby's bed so the stomach contents stay down. It is probably similar to what we call heart burn, which is very uncomfortable.

For reflux and silent reflux, you must see your GP so you can be prescribed the correct medication to reduce acid production or to neutralise the acid. There may also be an underlying problem e.g. weaker than usual valve to the stomach, lactose intolerance or something else so see your GP. Your GP can also prescribe hypo-allergenic milk formula (if it is the milk that is causing the problem), or if you are breast feeding you may need to change your diet.

If for any reason you think your baby is unwell or something is not normal, see your GP.

Summary

I hope you find this book helpful and if you follow some of my tips, you will have a calm and happy baby who plays well, eats well and sleeps well.

You and your baby will both know what is happening and what to expect. The first three months, I feel, are crucial. Start as you mean to go on, that way there are no bad habits made which you will then have to change.

To summarise:

Teach your baby to self-settle.

Encourage your baby to go 2½ to 3 hours between feeds and as they get older, then four hours.

Encourage them to eat well.

Teach them to play and amuse themselves.

Give lots of cuddles and chat.

Follow your baby's cues.

Once you have a routine in place and your baby is eating and sleeping well...

The rest will follow

Testimonials

Helen de Whitte:

'I have been extremely impressed by Fiona's work and have hugely appreciated her presence. Her extensive experience with babies and her confidence make her a very knowledgeable and experienced nurse. For all questions, big or small, she has solutions or ways to improve. Fiona has never been judgmental, which helps to gain confidence in our role as a new mum. I could not envision another baby without her on our side.'

Sophia Fafalios:

'The connection Fiona has with babies is something I personally have never seen before. Sometimes when they look at one another it feels like they are having a conversation in entirely their own language. This quickly becomes evident in the positive reaction that babies have to her, as they feel she understands them, which in turn makes them calmer. Her attitude to routine is equally respectful of the baby, as she is firm in certain elements of her routine but also provides a little flexibility in the right places, to take account each baby's mood and character.'

Delphine Steel:

'I have been very lucky to have Fiona as a maternity nurse for both of my boys. In my view she is the best you can expect from a maternity nurse, very gentle and calm. Her long experience and confidence with babies helps her put each baby in a routine with great ease. I think of her as a 'baby whisperer'; she understands instinctively what a baby needs/wants, and babies are always so happy with her. Both of my babies are in good routines and slept through the night at an early stage although they both had very different paths to get there. Fiona was sure to find out what worked for each of them.'

Selina Tollemache Hopkins:

'Fiona has considerable experience and was able to offer me very sound and helpful advice. She has shown considerable care and attention to detail while looking after our daughter and has been very flexible and adaptable in her approach to fitting in with our busy lives. We are very sad to see her go but she leaves us with a very happy and contented baby in a very good routine.'

Nina Shaw:

'As a result of Fiona's presence, we have become very knowledgeable and confident parents. Fiona also helped us to truly enjoy this special time with our newborn son. Fiona leaves us with all the necessary tools to understand the needs of our baby. Her repeat bookings and referrals are a testament to her sought after skills as a maternity nurse.'

Jackie Appel–malmaeus:

'Fiona is a great combination between structured and flexible. She never imposed her opinions or ways of doing things on us, but asked us what our goals were and offered suggestions taking great interest in our son's wellbeing. Fiona was able to ease him into a routine which allowed us all to get the rest we needed. Fiona is an outstanding maternity nurse. She is completely reliable professional responsible and punctual. We have always been confident that our son was in safe hands.'

Recommended Reading

Lynne Murray and Liz Andrews, 2005
'The Social Baby - Understanding babies' communication from birth'.
The Children's Project Ltd.

Marshall H Klaus, MD/Phyllis H Klaus, C.S.W.M.F.C.C., 1999
'Your Amazing Baby'.
Da Capo Press Books.

Vimala McClure, 2007
'Infant Massage – A handbook for loving parents'.
Souvenir Press Ltd.

Harvey Karpp, MD, 2003 –
'The Happiest Baby on the Block'.
Bantum Dell.

www.iaim.org.uk

www.lullabytrust.org.uk

www.yourbabyspa.com

www.fionacookeonline.co.uk

Index